HOW THINGS WORK

Notes on Economic Policy

Keith Quincy

UNIVERSITY
PRESS OF
AMERICA

Lanham • New York • London

Copyright © 1991 by

University Press of America®, Inc.

4720 Boston Way
Lanham, Maryland 20706

3 Henrietta Street
London WC2E 8LU England

Library of Congress Cataloging-in-Publication Data

Quincy, Keith, 1941-
How things work : notes on economic policy / by Keith Quincy.
p.   cm.
Includes bibliographical references and index.
1. United States—Economic policy.   I. Title.
HC106.3.Q88   1991
338.973—dc20   90–29182 CIP

ISBN 0–8191–8190–0 (alk. paper)

The paper used in this publication meets the minimum requirements of American National Standard for Information Sciences—Permanence of Paper for Printed Library Materials, ANSI Z39.48–1984.

For James Wallace

Acknowledgements

In addition to his usual and much appreciated encouragement and support, Professor James Wallace read an early draft of the book and offered valuable suggestions for improvement. I am also grateful to Professor Russell Snyder of the EWU economics department for graciously checking the manuscript for errors in theory and fact. He went over each page in detail and questioned me relentlessly until I got things right. Anna Quincy read several versions of the book and prodded me to express things clearly and in simple language. I should also like to thank countless past students of my Government 100 class for their many questions about economic policy, and especially for their unflagging interest in how things work and why they so often go wrong. I have used their questions as a guide for the topics in this book, and have tried to demystify economic policy as far as my talents permit.

Table of Contents

TABLE OF CONTENTS

Tables and Figures

Tables

Figures

Chapter 1

Faith in Free Markets

All advanced capitalist economies are mixed economies. Markets are to a large extent free, but there is also considerable government regulation, direction and control of the economy. In western Europe and Japan this is widely accepted as necessary. In America it is still a matter of considerable debate.

This mystifies many foreign observers who sometimes openly wonder how such a large capitalist country can afford to be so naive about the need for government management of the economy. Recently, European bankers and financiers have begun to warn investors away from the American economy because of the U.S. government's failure to properly regulate the American banking industry. There is also considerable astonishment that the U.S. has rejected the need for any sort of long range economic planning, what is commonly called an industrial policy. Some believe that without strong leadership from government the U.S. economy is destined to decline. As one foreign banker noted, "The United States is clearly no longer the dominant economic power. Over the next five years or more, it will be Europe that drives the world economy."[1]

Americans have seldom listened to advice from foreigners. The belief is widespread that we are special, and our values unique. Moreover, there is a strong tradition of hostility to government, especially when it tries to meddle with the economy. The debate over government involvement in the economy may have been settled abroad, but it still continues here and is far from settled.

For example, during his first presidential campaign Ronald Reagan pointed a finger at big government as the source of most of our economic woes and promised to reduce both its size and influence. In fact, once

Reagan became president he did very little to keep that promise. True, the decontrol of certain industries, like the airlines, begun during the Carter administration, was continued under Reagan. Also, in an effort to get government "off the back of business", Reagan encouraged and condoned lax enforcement of anti-trust laws as well as health and safety regulations and programs to clean up the environment. Nevertheless, on the whole, the federal government did more rather than less during Reagan's administration. For instance, the size of the federal budget grew to record proportions. This was in part due to a massive increase in spending for defense and, in time, to the need to accommodate the dramatic increase in the size of the interest payment on the national debt fueled by Reagan's record budget deficits. It was also due to the fact that many of the programs Reagan had targeted as fat in the federal budget survived his rhetoric without suffering serious cuts in funding. Indeed, even after all of Reagan's get tough talk about reducing welfare, the welfare system did not shrink out of sight but actually grew larger than ever before with millions of Americans benefiting from hefty increases in social security, medicare and medicaid payments. In sum, big government as measured by the size of the budget did not go away; it did not even get smaller; it actually grew.

TABLE 1
Average Annual Growth in GNP: US and USSR (1930s-1970s)

	1930s	1940s	1950s	1960s	1970s
US	- 2	5	3.9	4	2.8
Soviets	5	4	6	5.25	3.3

Sources: *Real World Macro* (Somerville, MA: Economic Affairs Bureau, 1989), p. 90; Marshal Goldman, *USSR in Crisis* (New York: W.W. Norton, 1983), p.47.; Robert Campbell, *Soviet Economic Power* (Boston: Houghton Mifflin, 1966), p. 123.

This did not effect Reagan's popularity. People liked his rhetoric even if it had little substance. Part of the reason seemed to be a widespread hostility toward government; but millions also appeared to share Reagan's faith in the power of free markets. If only we would let them operate unimpeded by government meddling, the economy would expand; affluence would spread across the land; and everything would be okay.

Is this faith in free markets justified? Are free markets the most powerful engine for economic growth ever devised? You might be surprised to learn that economic growth in communist systems has often been higher than in capitalist economies. For example, until quite recently, economic growth in the Soviet Union has, on average, exceeded that of the United States (see Table 1). This fact was ignored until the late 1950s when the Soviets launched Sputnik, the first man made satellite in space. The Soviet success in space was viewed as a demonstration of Russian technological and economic proficiency. While Soviet superiority in space technology caused alarm because of its implications for the arms race, the perception that the Soviets were also ahead of us in the economic race was a humbling embarrassment and one of the factors that prompted the Kennedy administration to design strategies for stimulating the American economy. In fact, the economy did grow dramatically during the Kennedy years. Even so, the U.S. was still unable to surpass Soviet economic growth until the late 1980s.[2] And by then the Soviets had already made good on Khrushchev's prediction of the early 1960s that his nation would one day out-produce the U.S. in certain vital sectors of the economy. And, indeed, by 1980 the Soviets were producing more steel, oil, coal, cement, lead, nickel, tractors, machine tools, and wheat than the U.S.[3]

While impressive, Soviet economic growth is also deceptive. The emphasis has been on heavy industry, large construction projects, and defense, rather than on consumer goods. Moreover, while the Soviets have historically set aside a higher percentage of their GNP (usually exceeding 30 percent per annum) for investment in their economy than capitalist states, they have not always invested wisely. During Stalin's reign, scientist and engineers were denied access to information about western technology. Unable to borrow ideas, they were forced to invent everything on their own. As a result, machinery in many industries was inefficient by western standards. Even after Stalin's death, when borrowing ideas from the west was finally tolerated and support for Soviet scientific and engineering research was greatly increased, the adoption of new technology to increase productivity was slow in coming. Soviet plant managers were always hesitant to innovate for fear of the unknown. By official consensus, a successful plant was one which met production quotas set by the central planning authority. Failure to meet a quota could result in a plant manager's demotion, or *even worse*. This created a disincentive to experiment with new technology. Perhaps new technology might increase productivity, but it might just as easily reduce output. After all, even successful innovations take time to work. In the meantime, production lags while workers and engineers struggle to work out the kinks in new procedures and equipment. Quotas remain unmet while these necessary adjustments are made, and many a promising career is placed in jeopardy. Consequently, even with extraordinary high levels of investment, the productivity of labor and machinery in the Soviet economy continued to lag behind average productivity in the industrialized economies of Europe and the U.S. In fact, the Soviets had to invest more than their capitalist rivals just to keep up, and increase investment even more to pull ahead.[4]

The capital to pay for decades of intensive development came from wages held back from Soviet workers and farmers who toiled for nearly two generations at subsistence pay. True, housing and food was heavily subsidized so that the cost of living was far lower in the Soviet Union than in the U.S.; but if that left the Soviets extra money to spend, they had little to spend it on. Shortages of even inferior goods were endemic to the system, which explains why so much of what was earned in wages wound up as savings—there was little to buy. In the end, decades of Soviet economic planning resulted in little real economic progress for average citizens. Indeed, for many the experience was of a continuously declining standard of living vis-a-vis the industrialized societies of the west. For example, before the revolution in 1917 Russia was ranked seventh in the world in per capita consumption. In 1990 it ranked behind South Africa at 77th.[5]

By the mid-1980s, it had become clear to a number of top Soviet leaders that it was no longer possible to deliver both guns and butter to Soviet citizens. Because of the economy's poor performance, a continued build-up in defense could be managed only by delaying indefinitely the long promised higher standard of living which the capitalist west now took for granted. There was even some question whether the lagging Soviet economy could support increased military spending in any case. Without an improved economy, there might not be either guns or butter. Gorbachev concluded there had to be economic reform. He set about to dismantle the old command economy inherited from Stalin and allow for more free enterprise. However, the process of economic reform has been unsteady and it is yet unclear whether the Soviets will be able to switch to free markets any time in the near future.

Whether or not the Soviets succeed in reforming their economy, one thing is clear—free markets possess important virtues which communist economies lack. The principal one is that free markets are better able to deliver the sort of goods and services people want. Free markets are consumer oriented, and it is generally the consumer who benefits when free markets are given considerable free reign.

NOTES

[1]Glenn Frankel, "The Worried View from Europe," *The Washington Post National Weekly Edition* (October 15-21, 1990), p. 8.

[2]Actually, CIA estimates placed the annual growth rate of the Soviet economy at about 1.9 percent between 1981 and 1985. This was only slightly lower than the U.S. figure at about 2.1 percent. In fact, the CIA estimate was wrong. The Soviets didn't do nearly that well. They may very well have experienced negative growth every year during that period. See Daniel Patrick Moynihan, "The Peace Dividend," *The New York Review of Books* (June 28,1990), p. 3.

3Marshal Goldman, *USSR in Crisis* (New York: W.W. Norton, 1983), p. 33.

4Vaclav Holesovsky, *Economic Systems: Analysis and Comparison* (New York: McGraw-Hill Book Company, 1977), pp. 312-316.

5David Remnick, "A Vast Landscape of Want," *The Washington Post National Weekly Edition* (May 28 - June 3, 1990), p.6.

Chapter 2
The Great Depression

Score a point for free markets. They produce what people want. But the delivery is not always steady. Capitalist economies often suffer violent ups and downs. The ups are usually accompanied by inflation, the downs by high unemployment. The worst down was the Great Depression of the 1930s. It lasted almost an entire decade, and if it hadn't been for the Second World War it might have lasted even longer. At the height of the depression nearly 25 percent of all workers were unemployed. Eighty-five thousand businesses failed. More than 9,000 banks closed. The economy shrank by more than one-third.

CAUSES

The reasons for the economy's collapse are still debated. Invariably, the stock market crash of 1929 is mentioned but other, more serious, problems were the high level of foreign debt, protective tariffs, and the unequal distribution of income.

1929 STOCK MARKET CRASH

It is a popular belief that the stock market crash of 1929 caused the depression. This is not strictly true. But it did make things worse than they needed to be. The crash was the result of excessive speculation, a growing bubble that was bound to burst. The reason why so many people suddenly began speculating in the stock market is not entirely clear. Perhaps it was misplaced confidence in the strength of the economy, or just simple greed. Whatever the reason, the urge to speculate by investors

great and small was given a mighty boost by a group of powerful
speculators with fortunes made in stocks, auto manufacturing, and grain
markets who purchased huge amounts of stock in 1928.[1] These speculators were banking on a big upturn in the economy, especially in autos
and radios, which were two big mass consumption items at the time.
Stock prices jumped in response to these huge stock purchases and
convinced many that the stock market was ready for a high and steady
climb. As others joined in the speculation, stock prices shot up further,
encouraging many to get in the market and earn hefty profits.

Buying On Margin

Lax regulations made it easy for anyone with a little money to get
into the speculation game. Stocks could be purchased on margin, that is
for a percent of their market value, usually for about 10 percent. That
meant a speculator could buy $10,000 worth of stock for as little as
$1,000. As often as not, even the initial $1,000 didn't come from the
speculator's own pocket but from a bank loan. The remaining $9,000 was
owed to the stockbroker who not only received a broker fee on the full
$10,000 but was also owed a hefty interest charge for the remaining
$9,000 which was treated as a loan. None of this concerned the speculator
very much because he counted on a rapid rise in the stock's value to get
him out of this mess with a nice profit to boot. Suppose the stock's value
increased to $15,000. The speculator could then sell his stock, pay off his
$9,000 debt to the stockbroker, and pocket the remaining $6,000. All this
for a mere investment of $1,000.

What made speculation so attractive was that so many people were
trying their hand at it. All these stock purchases kept driving the price of
stocks up, making speculation even more inviting. Another thing that kept
it going was that many banks were willing to loan money for speculation.
They did this because they had so much money on hand. This was the
fault of the Federal Reserve, the institution that oversees America's
banking system.

Help From the Federal Reserve

In 1927, two years before the stock market crash, the Federal Reserve agreed to help out the central banks of England and France. These banks were overextended, and didn't have enough reserves to meet loan demands. They asked the Federal Reserve to help out by lowering interest rates for American banks. Low interest rates would encourage English and French investors to borrow from banks in America rather than from banks in their own countries.

The Federal Reserve obliged by first lowering the interest rate on loans it made to banks searching for additional funds to lend out to customers. These banks responded by borrowing money from the Federal Reserve, increasing the funds available for loans. Then the Federal Reserve pumped additional money into the banking system by purchasing government securities (which banks regularly purchase as safe investments) from banks across the country, $340 million worth to be exact.[2]

With all that additional money in the banking system, interest rates on loans naturally declined. Unfortunately, a good deal of the new money went as loans to stockbrokers who in turn used the money to finance margin buying by speculators who could play the market even more easily now than before.

The Federal Reserve eventually became alarmed at so much money being loaned for speculation. It raised the rate on the money it loaned its member banks to make speculative buying more expensive. But this did almost nothing to quell the speculative passions of the stock buying public. Then the Federal Reserve warned member banks that they might not be able to borrow money from the Federal Reserve to loan out to their own customers if they continued making loans to stock brokers and speculators. This didn't work either, partly because a number of large banks simply ignored the warning and made loans to speculators anyway. And also because money was available elsewhere: some corporations with extra money on hand started making money available to speculators to cash in on the speculation frenzy.[3]

The Bubble Bursts

In late October 1929, the stock market was deluged with stock put up for sale by traders who had pushed their credit to the limit; they had waited too long for an upsurge in prices before selling their stock, and now had to find money to pay their margin calls. Stock prices tumbled and panicked stock owners began dumping their own stock before prices fell even further. In short, the bubble burst. Standard and Poor's composite index of stocks dropped in one day from 245 to 162. In that same day, $7 billion worth of bank loans to brokers and speculators became worthless. Eventually, as confidence in the stock market evaporated, the value of all stock listed on the New York Stock Exchange would plummet from a high of $89 billion in 1929 to a mere $17 billion in 1932.

Not only did average Americans lose faith in the stock market, reports of bank losses due to bad loans to speculators caused a rash of runs on banks. People wanted their money out while it was still there. Alas, it wasn't there. Banks never keep the full amount of their customer's deposits on hand. Only a small fraction is set aside, the rest is loaned out or invested. Many banks had to close their doors and declare bankruptcy. Banks continued to fail after the crash as the economy worsened (for reasons explained below) and more people and businesses defaulted on loans. By 1932, the money supply in the U.S. had shrunk by one-third.[4] But cheap money, and a lot of it, was one of the things needed to turn the economy around, to encourage people to reinvest in the economy and get it going again. Unfortunately, cheap money only appeared when it was too late, when faith in the economy was at an all-time low and pessimistic businessmen and investors wouldn't borrow no matter how low the interest rate.

FOREIGN DEBT

As for the collapse of the economy itself, government probably shares some of the blame. During the First World War, England and France had borrowed heavily from the U.S. to finance their war with Germany. After the war, their economies were sluggish and both countries asked the U.S. to forgive their combined debt of over $7 billion, funds which they believed could be put to better use in rebuilding their own economies. Calvin Coolidge was president at the time and he refused the request. It was not a smart move. England and France were important trading partners, and if paying the debt worsened their economies, they would be hard pressed to purchase our exports. Our own economy might soon be in trouble as well. And, indeed, it was.

TARIFFS

Another unwise decision occurred in 1930 with the passage of the Hawley-Smoot Tariff Act over the protest of many prominent American and European economists. Hawley-Smoot was the second major tariff act in less than eight years. The economy had expanded rapidly during the 1920s, but farmers didn't share in the rising wealth. Prices for their crops continued to fall. Many went bankrupt. The two tariff acts, mainly promoted by congressmen from farm states, taxed imported agricultural products with an eye to reducing supply and raising prices for domestic crops. The tariffs also extended to many manufactured goods as well. This had two consequences, one immediate and the other long term. The immediate consequence was retaliatory tariffs from many of America's trading partners. The brakes were applied to international trade. We stopped buying foreign goods, and they stopped purchasing our exports. Very quickly the economies of Europe and the U.S. began to contract. The other difficulty was that foreign firms had borrowed nearly $12 billion from American banks and corporations, and their ability to repay those loans depended on export sales to the U.S.[5] Now that this source of revenue was drying up, they had difficulty meeting their obligations. Things got very bad, very quickly.

UNEQUAL DISTRIBUTION OF INCOME

Government wasn't the only culprit. The economic boom of the 1920s did not benefit everyone equally. As already noted, farmers were left out, and at the time they constituted about 21 percent of the workforce. The majority of non-agricultural workers didn't fare much better because many businesses increased profits by holding down wages. For example, between 1920 and 1929 output per man hour increased 55 percent in manufacturing while wage rates in manufacturing increased by only 2 percent. During the same period, profits, interest and rent—the sort of income that goes to upper-income individuals—increased by 45 percent.[6] The rich were getting richer and the average worker was seeing little improvement in his or her income. Over time this skewed the distribution of income. Thirty percent of all income went to the top 2 percent of the population. The top forty percent earned a whopping 76 percent of all income. This meant that a majority of Americans (60 percent) had to make do with what was left. In short, income was concentrated at the top, and spread thin everywhere else.

This made recovery very difficult. Workers spend nearly all of their income. The wealthy hold back a large part in savings. When an economy is booming this savings reenters the economy because banks loan it out to investors who use it to purchase buildings, raw materials and equipment. On the other hand, when the economy sours, potential investors become anxious about future profits. Many delay investment decisions hoping the economy will get better and reduce the risk of losses. While they are waiting, the very funds needed to get the economy back on its feet remain in the banks.

The problem of unused savings might not have been so troublesome for the American economy in the 1930s if incomes had been more equally distributed. If most income was earned by workers, the amount of money leaking out of the economy into savings accounts would have been less.

Demand for products and services would never have dropped as far as it did because nearly all earned income would have become purchases of the economy's output. But workers didn't earn most of the nation's income, and when they became unemployed and ran quickly through their modest savings, they ceased being consumers and dropped out of the economy.

The result was one economic contraction after another. Things got so bad that banks couldn't get investors to borrow funds to stimulate the economy no matter how low the interest rate. With all that money languishing in the banks there was no hope that the economy would recover on its own. Free markets were supposed to automatically adjust to all conditions and guarantee economic health. What was the problem?

KEYNES

Up to that time, economists could offer no solution to the problem because they didn't really see it as a problem at all. Free markets were supposed to be self correcting. Economists assumed all money earned as income would reenter the economy as purchases of goods and services.

SAY'S LAW

This belief was long ago enshrined in *Say's Law*, an economic axiom named after the French economist Jean-Baptiste Say who, in his *Treatise on Political Economy* (*Traité d'Économie Politique*) published way back in 1803, had insisted supply always creates its own demand because the cost of producing something is always someone's income, whether it be wages to workers or profits to capitalists. According to Say, all of this income eventually becomes purchases, either directly when workers' wages go for food and lodging, or indirectly when the savings of capitalists is used or borrowed for investment in the economy. Consequently, the production of anything always creates its own demand: that is, the income to purchase it.

To prevent misunderstanding, Say allowed that workers in a particular industry may not purchase the goods they produce, just as capitalists do not always invest their profits in their own companies. But Say insisted this only means demand can become slack in one sector of the economy while growing stronger in another. Of course, this might cause minor recessions, but after adjustments are made and resources shuttled from areas of low to high demand, the economy will always even out in the end.

In any case, the point Say wanted to stress is that production produces the necessary overall demand to purchase all goods produced. And because supply creates its own demand, major recessions generated by insufficient demand are an impossibility. So convincing was the proposition that supply creates its own demand that some, like the English economist Stanley Jevons, claimed that a general depression was "absurd and self-contradictory."[7]

LEAKAGES

It took a maverick British economist, John Maynard Keynes, to realize that a good deal of income could leak out of an economy and stay locked up in savings accounts in banks for a long time. Keynes argued that people of low to moderate means spend nearly all their income. However, as one's income grows, some of it is set aside as savings. People with very high incomes save a lot, those with low incomes spend nearly everything they earn and save very little. In technical terms, this means that, unlike the poor, the rich have a low marginal propensity to consume. Less of every additional dollar they earn goes to consumption and more goes into savings.

Keynes pointed out that this doesn't cause problems in good times because investors borrow this savings to reinvest in the economy. This investment translates into purchases of equipment and machinery or additional goods and services. In short, in good times nearly all income earned is used for some kind of consumption—just as Say had predicted. There is sufficient demand to prevent the economy from contracting and to keep workers employed. But when times are bad, and investors become cautious, a good deal of savings is not borrowed. It remains in banks as lost demand. Because this savings has "leaked" out of the economic system, there is not enough money to purchase all of the output of the economy. Unemployment rises. Laid off workers run through their meager savings, and then drop out of the economy. Since they are no longer purchasing goods and services, demand drops further and businesses have to lay off more workers. The economy continues to contract, spiraling downward. Unless investors change their minds and tap into savings, the recession could become a depression. And unless a new source of purchasing power can be created, the depression may persist for a very long time.

THE IMPORTANCE OF DEFICIT SPENDING

Keynes recommended deficit spending by government as the only feasible source of much needed purchasing power to end a depression. He also observed it doesn't matter what government purchases. It can contract with firms to dig holes and fill them up again. The important thing is to get people working, put money in their pockets so they can make purchases of their own. Eventually, this increase in demand will stimulate business borrowing for investment, precisely what is needed to soak up the money in savings accounts that has leaked out of the system.

In sum, Keynes argued that insufficient demand is the principal cause of depressions. The obvious solution is to increase demand. However, since so much money is locked up in savings and has essentially leaked out of the economy, government must step in. For when investors no longer invest, only government can take up the slack by increasing total, or aggregate, demand through government spending. Government spending creates incomes for workers, income that will be spent on goods and services. This will increase aggregate demand and help get the economy back on its feet again.

So Keynes' advice to end the depression was to increase government spending. Just how much government spending would be required to end the depression and return the economy to full employment was unclear, but Keynes was certain it would have to be monumental in scale to do the trick.

NOTES

[1]Frederick Lewis Allen, "The Bull Market and the Crash of '29," in Paul Samuelson, Robert Bishop and John Coleman (eds.), *Readings in Economics* (New York: McGraw-Hill Book Company, Inc., 1958), p. 171.

[2]John Kenneth Galbraith, *Money: Whence It Came, Where It Went* (Boston: Houghton Mifflin, 1975), p. 175; William Greider, *Secrets of the Temple* (New York: Simon & Schuster Inc., 1987), pp. 296-300.

[3]Frederick Lewis Allen, "The Bull Market and the Crash of '29," pp. 174-176.

[4]William Greider, *Secrets of the Temple*, p. 299.

[5]Jude Wanniski, *The Way the World Works* (New York: Simon and Schuster, 1978), p. 128.

[6]Gilbert Burck and Charles Silberman, "What Caused the Great Depression," in Morton Grossman et al. (eds.), *Readings in Current Economics* (Homewood, Illinois: Richard D. Irwin, Inc., 1958), p. 81.

[7]Robert L. Heilbroner, *The Worldly Philosophers* (New York: Simon and Schuster, 1961), p. 149.

Chapter 3
Roosevelt

Keynes' *The General Theory of Employment, Interest and Money* wasn't published until 1936, midway into the depression. Keynes' ideas shook the world of academic economics but had minimal effect on economic policies. Franklin Roosevelt was elected president of the United States in 1932 with a pledge to end the depression. However, following the conventional wisdom he supported a balanced budget and retreated from increased government spending whenever the federal deficit grew very large. Not that he was inactive. Quite the contrary, he expanded government enormously. But the scope of his programs was never large enough to seriously increase aggregate demand.

REBUILDING THE ECONOMY

To get the economy going again Roosevelt believed it would first be necessary to restructure the economy. There needed to be cooperation rather than conflict between business and labor. Businessmen had to have greater confidence, and an expectation of certain profits. The financial system needed reforming so that depositors would regain their lost faith in banks. Markets in agriculture needed to be restructured to guarantee adequate prices for farmers. And the unemployed had to be put to work.

NATIONAL INDUSTRY RECOVERY ACT

In the beginning, Roosevelt was generous with business. This was to be expected. For over a hundred years the federal government had tried to help business with subsidies and protective legislation. Rarely, and then only after much agitation from an outraged public, did the government attempt to regulate business for the public interest. Indeed, the narrow and often short-sighted interests of corporate America were pretty much equated with the national interest.

Subsidies for business occurred in many forms. Early in the 19th century, roads and canals were built at public expense, primarily to reduce the transportation costs of businesses and expand their markets. After the Civil War, western ranchers were granted access to public lands for grazing their cattle. Dams were constructed to provide cheap electric energy for urban areas and factories. The dams were also used for the irrigation of farms, turning worthless arid lands into some of the most productive agriculture areas in the world.

Sometimes the subsidies were shamelessly direct. In the 1870s, the railroads were given public money to expand their lines all the way to the Pacific Ocean. In addition to money, the railroads were given public lands to sell to raise capital for expansion. In total acreage, the extent of public land transferred to the railroads was almost twice the size of Texas.

Protective legislation was mainly through tariffs on imported goods to protect domestic industry and agriculture from foreign competition. Immigration laws were also used to help business. Until 1927, the U.S. maintained an open door policy on immigration, guaranteeing a seemingly endless supply of cheap labor that kept industrial wages low and corporate profits high.

In line with this tradition of government support of business, one of Roosevelt's first acts after taking office was to engineer the passage of the National Industry Recovery Act (NIRA). The legislation was popular with big business because it emphasized cooperation over competition. What this meant is that executives of large corporations could cut deals, set prices, and control labor without being charged with violations of anti-trust laws. The idea was to allow corporations to form cartels, fix prices, and earn high profits with the hope that this would encourage them to expand production and rehire the unemployed. Corporate executives considered this legislation an unusual display of wisdom. Small businessmen, however, were of a different mind. They weren't included in this new cooperative capitalism and promptly labeled it government sponsored monopoly. They didn't have to worry. The NIRA didn't last very long. It was declared unconstitutional by the Supreme Court in 1935.

BANKS AND THE STOCK MARKET

Legislation was also passed to bolster confidence in the banking system. Thousands of banks had already failed, many others were teetering toward collapse. The problem was anxious depositors. When a lot of them withdrew their funds from a bank because they questioned its solvency, the run on the bank became a self-fulfilling prophecy. The bank seldom had enough funds to cover all the withdrawals and had to close its doors. The exception was the mutual savings banks. Run by their depositors, they maintained high reserves and made extremely safe investments. Depositor confidence in them was therefore very high. Few failed. But mutual savings banks were a small fraction of the banking industry. Most other banks did not enjoy the public confidence of the mutual savings banks and needed help to improve their image. To prevent bank runs, the Banking Act of 1933 created the Federal Deposit Insurance Corporation (FDIC) which insured individual deposits in member banks[1] for up to $2,500. Now if a bank had insufficient funds to pay back depositors, the federal government made up the difference.

Something was also done for the stock market. Existing banking laws were amended to bar banks from the securities business; they could no longer participate in margin buying. In 1933, the Securities Act established harsh penalties for brokers who failed to reveal all relevant facts about securities they sold. And the Securities and Exchange Act of 1934 set up the Securities and Exchange Commission to oversee the stock market and set regulations in the public interest. The same act also gave the Federal Reserve the power to set margin requirements on all stock deals.[2]

FARMERS AND DEBTORS

Roosevelt also tried to help farmers with the Agricultural Adjustment Act. The object of this legislation was to reduce the supply of agricultural products and, thus, increase their price. This would raise the incomes of farmers. The principle technique used for crop reduction was to pay farmers to reduce the amount of acreage they cultivated. A controversial measure employed during the first year of the act to give immediate relief to cotton and pig farmers was to order 10 million acres of cotton plowed under and 6 million pigs slaughtered. The object, of course, was to reduce supply and raise prices but many, including farmers themselves, saw it as simply wasteful.

Another move to help farmers, and debtors, was Roosevelt's devaluation of the dollar. America was then on the gold standard which meant dollars could be redeemed for gold. The exchange rate was set at $20.63 per ounce. Roosevelt raised the rate to $35 per ounce, which meant that a dollar purchased less gold than before, losing about 40 percent of its former value. This led to rising prices because producers had to charge more to get the same value as before. Higher prices was just what farmers wanted for their crops. Debtors liked the change, too, because they could pay back loans in cheaper dollars. In essence, they now owed lenders 40 percent less.

Devaluation of the dollar disturbed the business and banking community and was the beginning of growing business hostility toward Roosevelt and his New Deal. This hostility only increased when he tried to help the poor and unemployed. To many businessmen and conservatives it seemed like socialism had come to the United States. Ironically, from the Keynesian perspective, Roosevelt's relief programs offered the best chance of bringing America out of the depression and saving capitalism in American. These programs increased aggregate demand by purchasing goods and services from private firms and by putting paychecks in the pockets of millions of the unemployed, paychecks that translated into increased demand for goods and services. The problem was that Roosevelt never went far enough.

JOBS AND SPENDING

The newly created Civil Works Administration (CWA) gave jobs to 4 million people building a half-million miles of roads. The CWA also built schools, 40,000 in all, and 1,000 airports. It pumped over a billion dollars into the economy. This was mostly accomplished through deficit spending which the business community considered irresponsible. After loud protests of fiscal irresponsibility, Roosevelt backed down. The CWA was disbanded in the spring of 1934.

A smaller program, the Public Works Administration (PWA), replaced the CWA. Under its auspices bridges and harbors were constructed, ships built for the navy, planes manufactured for the airforce, and low cost housing erected to replace substandard dwellings in city slums. It had a modest effect on unemployment, but barely affected aggregate demand.

The Civilian Conservation Corps (CCC) was another modest program that employed young men between the ages of 18 and 25 in flood control, and park and road construction. It would eventually give jobs to over 2 million unemployed. Many CCC projects survive, some in the Pacific Northwest. For example, Riverside State Park, located on the banks of the Spokane river just outside Spokane, Washington, was constructed by the CCC in the late 1930s. The park remains a popular attraction for Spokane residents and tourists.

A larger program, begun in 1935, was the Works Progress Administration (WPA). It employed nearly 2 million workers a year on various projects, like building roads, libraries, airports and golf courses. However, the wages paid were low, too low to significantly increase demand for goods in the private sector.

EASING THE PAIN

By 1935, it was pretty clear that government was losing the battle to end the depression. Roosevelt decided if he couldn't end it, at least he could make it a little less painful. It also signalled Roosevelt's growing disenchantment with the business community, a recognition that the business mentality not only did not provide solutions for ending the depression, it was part of the problem.

WELFARE

The first major step in easing the pain of the Depression occurred when Congress passed the Social Security Act. It gave pension benefits to older workers, created unemployment compensation to help the unemployed, and started a modest program of federal aid to families with dependent children. Other than some earlier pension plans for war veterans, the Social Security Act was the federal government's first serious attempt to provide welfare for American citizens.

LABOR

Labor unions were given a shot in the arm with the National Labor Relations Act (NLRA) which guaranteed labor's right to organize. The Act also established the Labor Relations Board to insure that this right was honored by business. Unions had fallen on hard times. Membership had declined from a high of around 5 million in 1925 to about 3.5 million in 1929. Part of the reason was discord within the union movement itself. The largest and most powerful labor union, the American Federation of Labor (AFL), was essentially a craft union, representing skilled rather than unskilled workers. Other unions, like the United Mine Workers, represented unskilled workers. Many labor organizers realized that unless skilled and unskilled workers joined ranks, it would be difficult to bargain effectively with employers who could always play one group off against

the other.   In 1935, some of the more radical members of the AFL bolted
from the parent organization to form the Congress of Industrial Organizations (CIO) as an industry-wide union including both skilled and
unskilled workers in steel, automobile manufacturing and rubber.   Eventually, the long standing enmity between skilled and unskilled labor was
partly resolved in 1955 when the AFL merged with the CIO to form the
AFL-CIO.   It is doubtful this would have occurred so soon without the
boost the NLRA gave to organized labor.

Prior to the New Deal, labor rejected politics as a way to improve
its position in the economy.   For the AFL, it was a matter of political
philosophy.   Ideologically it was as much opposed to government inter-
vention in the economy as was business.   The AFL did not seek legislation
benefiting workers or their unions, and spoke out strongly against such
legislation when it was proposed.[3]   And because of past experience, unions
representing unskilled laborers were suspicious of government which had
often sided with business against labor, sometimes even using federal
troops to break strikes.

Labor's refusal to use politics to advance its goals placed it at a
disadvantage with business which never hesitated to lobby government to
promote its interests.   Fortunately for labor, Roosevelt had appointed a
social worker, Frances Perkins, as his Secretary of Labor rather than a
high official from the AFL.   Perkins didn't share Labor's hostility to
government and didn't stand in the way of the NLRA which went far to
rectify the imbalance in power between labor and business.[4]   Indeed, the
Act provided the labor movement the government support it needed to get
moving again.   Union membership grew rapidly, much to the conster-
nation of business.

CONFRONTING POWER

While the National Industry Recovery Act had supported the idea
of business cartels, the 1935 Public Utility Holding Company Act attacked
concentrated economic power.   Roosevelt had decided that businesses with
too much power couldn't be trusted to serve the public interest.   He

singled out the utility companies to set an example and to stand as a warning.

TAKING ON THE UTILITY HOLDING COMPANIES

Holding companies are clever devices for the inexpensive control of large segments of an industry. They are usually pyramid arrangements. A holding company is formed and purchases controlling shares of stock (about 10 to 20 percent) in several companies. It now controls their operations. Other holding companies are formed to take over additional firms. Then a master holding company is formed to purchase controlling stock in these holding companies. It now controls them all, holding companies and the companies they control alike. Depending on the size of the pyramid, the master holding company can control an entire industry for a small fraction (one or two percent) of its total stock value. By 1935, twelve holding companies controlled 50 percent of all hydroelectric power in the United States; and they used that control to keep utility charges high and restrict electricity to high usage areas, which meant mostly to cities with large populations. Rural America had almost no electricity at all. The Public Utility Holding Act established a commission to oversee these holding companies, and to dissolve any of them if it was deemed they were not serving the public interest. Many were dissolved, and replaced by public rather than private utilities. For the first time many rural areas began to receive electricity.

Washington Water Power in Spokane, Washington is an example of a private utility that barely survived the Public Utility Holding Act. The company had been under the control of a holding company headquartered in New York City since 1895 when it was taken over by another holding company, American Power and Light, in 1928. American Power and Light was one of the holding companies dissolved by the Public Utility Holding Company Act, though it took seventeen years of court battles to sort out who actually owned Washington Water Power after the dissolution. During that period, Washington Water Power fought for its life as private utility companies throughout the state were replaced by public utilities. It survived three attempts in the 1940s to turn it into a public utility, and in 1955 it competed head-to-head with a public utility to decide which best served users in Stevens county. Stevens county voters chose Washington Water Power over the public utility and WWP became the sole utility provider in the county, making it the only private utility company in the state to replace a public utility with voter approval.[5]

TAX REFORM

Breaking up the holding companies was popular with rural America and with many average Americans who by now had lost considerable faith in business' ability to automatically generate prosperity. Schemes to soak the rich with higher income and corporate taxes were also becoming popular. In fact, during its short history, the income tax had mostly been a tax on the rich. President Lincoln had tried to finance the Civil War with an income tax only to have it declared unconstitutional by the Supreme Court. The Supreme Court did the same in 1895 when it struck down an income tax provision of a 1892 tariff act. The hostility of the Supreme Court ceased to be a problem after 1912 when the Sixteenth Amendment was ratified, giving the federal government the power to tax personal and corporate income.

The first income tax legislation was passed in 1913, and it levied a modest 1 percent tax on all individual and corporate income over $4,000. Since the level of this personal deduction was several times higher than the average income in America, the tax excluded nearly everyone but businesses and the very wealthy. The tax rate was raised to 10 percent in 1916, and then dramatically increased again in 1917 to generate revenue to support America's entrance into the First World War. The top rate on individuals was raised to 83 percent, and an excess profits tax on business funnelled all corporate profits over 8 percent into government coffers. By 1918, the income taxes of businesses and wealthy individuals were supplying nearly all federal revenues. Average Americans paid almost nothing. During the 1920s, pressures from business and the support of Republican presidents resulted in numerous amendments in the tax code, lowering the top rate for the rich, providing loopholes for businesses to reduce or eliminate their tax liability, and deleting the excess profits tax altogether.

In 1935, Roosevelt jumped on the soak-the-rich bandwagon and got Congress to raise the top income tax rate to 79 percent. An excess profits tax was also reinstated over violent opposition from business. Business kept up the opposition and Congress finally dropped the excess profits tax in 1938. Congress was also interested in changing the nature of the income tax. Up to then it was still more or less a tax on the upper class. Only 3.9 percent of the population paid income taxes in 1939, a small fraction of income earning Americans. In the 1940, Congress was able to override Roosevelt's veto and change the income tax from a tax on the rich to a tax on average Americans by lowering the personal exemption beneath the old $4,000 limit. It continued to lower it every year until, by 1945, 42.6 million Americans were paying income taxes. The effort to reduce the tax liability of the rich did not cease with this victory. Loopholes were continually added to the tax code. In the mid-1960s it took 1,100 pages to cite them all.[6] Not surprisingly, between 1952 and 1986, the effective federal tax rate for the richest 1 percent of tax payers declined from 32.2 to 22.1 percent.[7]

A COMMAND ECONOMY?

Despite Roosevelt's efforts—public works programs, welfare measures, the attack on economic concentration, and tax reform—the depression lingered. Indeed, in 1937 Roosevelt made matters worse. A year earlier the federal deficit had risen to $10 billion. Roosevelt was advised by his Secretary of the Treasury, Henry Morgenthau, that the budget deficit was too large and cuts needed to be made. Roosevelt complied. When Keynes heard of the move he immediately predicted the economy would contract. And that is just what it did. It wasn't until 1939 that Roosevelt finally conceded that conventional economic wisdom and business community fears of large deficits were not to be trusted. By then, it had become a moot point. Whether he liked it or not, Roosevelt was going to apply Keynesian principles to the economy in a big way.

U.S. entry into the Second World War brought an end to the depression and massive unemployment. The government had no choice but to engage in unprecedented deficit spending to gear up for the war. Prior to the war, Roosevelt's deficit spending never amounted to more than a small fraction of 1 percent of the Gross National Product—hardly measurable. In 1940, the deficit climbed to 3 percent of GNP. It jumped to 4.3 percent the next year, and by 1943 it had risen to an incredible 31.1 percent of GNP. The huge budget deficits of the Reagan administration are piddling by comparison. The largest, occurring in 1985, was $212 billion—only 5.4 percent of GNP.[8]

As Keynes had predicted, massive deficit spending launched the American economy on an upward path of rapid growth. Between 1939 and 1945, GNP increased by 189 percent. During that same period, unemployment declined from 17.2 to 1.9 percent. Of course, this was not exactly a fair test of Keynesian economics. Government did not just stimulate the economy through deficit spending, it pretty much dictated what was produced, and fixed wages and prices to keep down inflation. Most consumer goods were tightly rationed. Corporations involved in war production were guaranteed profits. In many respects it was a command economy. What distinguished it from the Soviet economy was that ownership of property still remained in private hands, though government often determined how it was to be employed. If it was capitalism, it was a strange sort of capitalism where markets weren't very free.

Could capitalism be saved only by altering it beyond recognition? Few were willing to consider the possibility. It was presumed government management of the economy would cease with the end of the war. After all, the only reason business tolerated massive deficit spending and price controls, or labor tolerated fixed wages, or consumers condoned rationing was patriotic support for the war effort. When that disappeared, so would the legitimacy of these policies. So the real test for Keynesian principles lay in the future.

NOTES

[1]Banks became members by agreeing to pay a nominal annual insurance premium for membership.

[2]Poyntz Tyler (ed.), *Securities, Exchanges and the SEC* (New York: H. W. Wilson Company, 1965), p. 153.

[3]Grant McConnell, *Private Power and American Democracy* (New York: Alfred A. Knopf, 1967), p. 83.

[4]Henry Pelling, *American Labor* (Chicago: University of Chicago Press, 1960), p. 162.

[5]Steve Blewett, *A History of The Washington Water Power Company, 1889-1989* (Spokane, WA: The Washington Water Power Company, 1989), pp. 33-47.

[6]Elliot Brownlee, "The American Way," *The Wilson Quarterly* (Spring 1989), p. 95.

[7]Joseph Pechman, *Tax Reform*, 2nd ed. (Washington, D.C.: The Brookings Institution, 1989), p. 22.

[8]*Real World Macro*, 6th ed. (Somerville, MA: Economic Affairs Bureau, Inc., 1989), p. 94.

Chapter 4
Post-War Economy

The adjustment to a peacetime economy was not as painful as some feared it might be. Keynesian economists predicted that without continued high deficit spending, transferred from defense to non-defense projects, the economy would experience a severe recession and high unemployment. Events did not bear them out. True, the GNP declined about 20 percent the first year, but unemployment only rose two percentage points. Then the economy began to grow despite the fact that the government held deficits below pre-war levels until 1950 when the deficit grew to a modest 1.2 percent of GNP.

UNEXPECTED STRENGTH

SAVINGS AND DEMAND

Two reasons are often cited to explain the unexpected strength of the economy. One is the high savings rate during the war. Because so many resources had been diverted to war production, normal consumer goods were in short supply. There was also mandatory rationing. No matter how much a person earned, there was only so much a family was allowed to buy. So unspent income went into savings. For example, in 1945 the average savings rate was a whopping 25 percent (it is less than 4 percent now). Rationing also generated what economists describe as pent-up demand. After denying themselves so much for so long, consumers had a long wish list of things they wanted to purchase. So Americans went on a buying binge when rationing ended. And because of the high rate of savings during the war years, they had plenty of money to spend once they got the chance.

AUTOS AND SUBURBS

Increased consumption was also aided by major demographic changes. For example, ownership of automobiles climbed dramatically, from 26 million in 1945 to 40 million in 1950, and up to 60 million by 1959. A major reason for the rising demand for automobiles was the growth of suburbia. A larger proportion of the population was living in suburbs and commuting to work in the cities. This new lifestyle made the automobile a necessity rather than a luxury. The auto industry began to grow rapidly, providing employment for millions of workers in automobile factories and in related industries like oil, rubber and road construction.

NEW CREDIT MARKETS

One reason people were moving to the suburbs in such large numbers was government sponsored housing loans which made home ownership affordable for millions. Today we take FHA and VA loans for granted, but prior to the New Deal housing loans were difficult to get and very expensive. This was because banks didn't like making home loans. For one thing, there was no secondary market for them. That is, there were no institutions interested in purchasing home loans from the banks and marketing them to investors. This meant banks had to hold on to the loans until they were paid off. Because of this, as late as the 1920s few banks offered home buyers long term loans. Usually the term of the loan was limited to a few years, and with no monthly payments. The entire principal and interest on the loan was due at the end of three or five years.

It wasn't until the late 1920s and early 1930s that home loans could be paid off in monthly installments instead of one lump sum. Nevertheless, for most people this wasn't much of an improvement. Because banks considered home loans a bad investment, they charged higher than normal interest rates to borrowers. And to limit risk, a bank never covered the full value of the home. Usually the loan covered only half of the purchase price. To finance the remaining half, a buyer had to take out a second and third mortgage, each at an even higher interest rate than the previous mortgage because there was less collateral left in the home and the risk to the bank of losing its investment was correspondingly greater should a default occur.

Under such conditions, working class families, and many families with middle class incomes, could not afford to finance a new home. The Roosevelt administration tried to rectify this with two pieces of legislation. The first was the Home Owner's Loan Corporation Act of 1933 which established the Savings and Loan Association charged with creating savings and loan banks across the country specializing in home loans. The second piece of legislation was the National Housing Act of 1934. The Act created the Federal Housing Administration (FHA) which provided a government guarantee of home loans made by savings and loan banks. If a borrower defaulted on a home loan, FHA would pay off the remaining debt. Shortly after this, the Veterans Administration (VA) established a similar program for military veterans, promising to pay off housing loans made to veterans should they default. With the risk taken out of FHA and VA loans, banks were willing to lower interest rates making it easier for people to afford suburban housing.

In order to further strengthen the home loan market, the Federal National Mortgage Association—known in real estate and banking circles as Fannie Mae—was created in 1938. Fannie Mae's sole purpose was to purchase FHA and VA mortgages from banks and sell them on the open market. The mortgages were attractive to investors because they were risk free. After all, the government guaranteed payment on the loans in case of default. And usually they provided a competitive interest rate. If they didn't, Fannie Mae could sell them at a discount. This is how it works. Suppose Fannie Mae has purchased a $70,000 mortgage yielding 12 percent interest for thirty years with monthly payments of about $720 per month. Also suppose that interest rates have gone up some, to about 12.2 percent. Suddenly, the mortgage is not so attractive at the lower 12 percent rate of return. To make it more attractive, Fannie Mae can discount it from its $70,000 face value to, say, $69,000. As it turns out, a monthly return of $720 is what you would get on a $69,000 mortgage at a 12.2 rate of interest. So for an investor purchasing the mortgage for $69,000, the actual rate of return would be very competitive. Of course, Fannie Mae would have lost $1,000 in the transaction, a small government subsidy to strengthen the housing market.

By creating a secondary market for home mortgages Fannie Mae made home mortgages more liquid. Banks could quickly transform them into dollars by selling them to Fannie Mae. The importance of this was that it provided banks a relatively constant supply of funds for home loans. A loan could be made, sold to Fannie Mae, and the proceeds used for more loans. Without a secondary market, most banks serving the housing market would have their money tied up in existing long term home loans. The volume of home loans they could make would be very limited. But with a secondary mortgage market, the volume could remain relatively high more or less indefinitely—a good deal for home buyers desperate for financing.

Actually, the New Deal housing legislation didn't have much of an impact at first because during the depression most people couldn't afford homes no matter how easy the financing. Moreover, it wasn't until after the war that the financing became really attractive. In the mid-1930s, FHA loans required a 20 percent down payment. Far too steep for most average families. However, after the war, the required down payment was progressively lowered until, in 1954, it dropped to a mere 3 percent. In that same year, VA loans required no down payment at all. Mortgage interest rates weren't that high either. In the mid-fifties they averaged about 5.5 percent. With the average price of a new home at $12,000, the monthly payment on a thirty year loan with no down payment was only $68.13. For many people, owning a house in the suburb was cheaper than paying rent for an apartment in the city.[1]

Millions joined the stampede to home ownership in suburbia. From 1948 to 1958, thirteen million homes were built in the U.S., 85 percent in the new suburbs. Each year more than a million acres of farmland was plowed under to make way for the new homes.

BABY BOOM

Perhaps as important as low interest loans was the rising birth rate, the baby boom, which encouraged many to make the move to suburbia. With more families having children, and the growing belief that cities were not a good place to raise them, the demand for suburban homes skyrocketed.

Sadly, one reason people found cities a bad places to raise families was racism. For nearly forty years Blacks had been migrating from grinding rural poverty in the south to northern industrial cities where there were jobs. The influx accelerated during war time when labor was in scarce supply. Blacks who might have suffered job discrimination in peacetime were simply too valuable to be turned away by managers of defense plants desperate for workers to man their assembly lines. Indeed, the flow of Black migrants from the south to the eastern seaboard, Great Lakes, and west coast was greater in total population than the influx of any single group of European immigrants before the First World War. Nearly "three-fourths of the population growth in New York, Pennsylvania, Ohio, Illinois, Michigan, and the District of Columbia between 1910 and 1940 was attributable to the arrival of black migrants."[2] Confronted with such a large numbers of Blacks threatening to become neighbors, many northern whites fled the city for the suburbs where for decades restrictive covenants made neighborhoods all white communities and an unspoken commitment from bank loan officers to deny mortgages to "undesirables" prevented Blacks and other minorities from joining suburbia.

Of course, few whites openly admitted this was the reason for the move. Instead it was the children. Every family had lots of them, and the suburb was portrayed in books and magazines, movies and the radio as the place to raise them properly. Indeed, the number of new children was unprecedented. For the eleven years between 1954 and 1964, four million new babies were born annually. Eventually the baby boomers would increase to a total of 75 million, nearly forty percent of the entire population. Indeed, in 1964 there were more children under fourteen than the entire population of the U.S. in 1881.[3]

Whole new markets for children opened up. They were the first generation of children to be specifically singled out by Madison Avenue as an identifiable market. "From the cradle, the baby boomers [were] surrounded by products created especially for them, from Silly Putty to Slinkys to skateboards."[4] Revenue for diaper companies nearly doubled in ten years. Toy sales doubled, year after year. Cowboy outfits alone became a $75 million industry. Baby food became a big industry with 1.5 billion cans sold in 1953 alone. Construction of new schools became a big business. In 1952, nearly 50,000 new classrooms were constructed throughout the nation. In the same year, Los Angeles alone was spending $1 million per week on new schools, and still it could not keep up with demand.[5]

EXPORTS

With expanding markets in autos, homes, and goods for infants and children, the economy grew quickly even without the support of high levels of government spending. However, not only did domestic consumption rise sharply after the war, so did foreign demand for U.S. goods. By 1948 the U.S. was responsible for 25 percent of all world trade and produced nearly one half of all manufactured goods. America produced 57 percent of the world's steel, 62 percent of all oil, and 80 percent of the world's automobiles. In short, the U.S. emerged from the war as the world's foremost industrial power.

On the other hand, America's competitors—West Germany, France, Italy, England, and Japan—were still recovering from the ravages of the war. During the fighting, their factories had been bombed into rubble, either by German or American bombers. In addition, the occupation of eastern and part of central Europe by the Soviet Union had cut off western Europe from its traditional source of relatively cheap raw materials—oil from Romania, coal, pigs and potatoes from Poland, and grain from Hungary, Poland, Romania and East Germany.[6]

Western Europe was in desperate need of funds to rebuild its factories and to purchase raw materials from new sources, such as the U.S. America came its aid. Named for Truman's Secretary of State, George Marshall, who administered the program, the Marshall plan provided $12 billion for the economic recovery of western Europe. The plan was as much an expression of self-interest as of altruism. The nations of western Europe had been our major trading partners. If they couldn't get their economies going again, they wouldn't be able to purchase our exports.

At the time, it didn't occur to anyone that once these nations rebuilt their economies they might do more than merely earn enough to purchase our exports. They might become formidable competitors. Indeed, over the years there were clear signs that this was occurring, though the U.S. government and major American corporations chose to ignore them. It would prove to be a costly mistake.

Consider Japan. When the Japanese began rebuilding their industry they tried to modernize wherever possible, employing the latest technology. Much of this new technology was developed by American scientists and engineers but was nevertheless shunned by American corporations because it was thought too costly to upgrade plants and equipment to make use of it. By 1957, Japan not only had the most modern steel mills, it had become the foremost producer of steel in the world. A year earlier Japan had already replaced Britain as the world's leading builder of ships.[7]

The Japanese relied heavily on American technological expertise to rebuild its economy. American engineers designed some of the first Japanese cars, and Japanese commitment to quality products was in large part made possible by an American expert on quality control, Edwards Deming. Ironically, the big American manufacturers ignored Deming and his revolutionary techniques for improving machine tolerances until they were nearly perfect. But the Japanese listened to him, published his books, and hired him as a consultant.[8] As much as anyone else, it was Deming who taught the Japanese how to make their cars better than those manufactured in the U.S. Today, the Deming Prize for quality manufacturing is one of the most prestigious awards in Japanese industry. Deming is famous in Japan. Most Americans have never heard of him.

While American automobile manufacturers actually reduced quality to increase profit margins, Japanese automakers increased quality while also cutting costs through more efficient manufacturing and quality control techniques. The Japanese were selling a better quality, lower priced car than the Americans. This presented a serious challenge to American auto makers. Nevertheless, even by the mid-1960s American auto companies openly doubted the Japanese could ever capture more than 5 percent of the American car market. And if they did, American car makers boasted they would strike back and destroy them.

By 1968, auto imports had captured 10 percent of the American market, with the Japanese accounting for nearly half of that figure. Detroit finally tried to fight back by producing a line of small cars, but they were poorly made and overpriced. The Japanese share of the market continued to grow until, by 1979, it accounted for 25 percent of the U.S. market. By the early 1980s, the Japanese had increased their share to 30 percent. Ford Motor Company finally came to its senses and hired Edwards Deming to teach Ford quality control. Still the Japanese surged ahead. In 1982, Honda began producing cars in America, in Marysville, Ohio. By 1985, the plant manufactured more cars than American Motors, making a Japanese automaker the fourth largest auto manufacturer in America.[9]

Former customers of America's industrial products were now major suppliers of the goods we purchased. However, in the decade after the war, few Americans imagined this possibility. The American economy seemed so strong it was difficult to conceive any competitor matching, let alone defeating, it in head-to-head competition.

LEGITIMIZATION OF KEYNESIAN ECONOMICS

Because of the strength of the post-war economy, it seemed to many that the economy didn't need government supervision to prosper.

Nevertheless, Keynesian economic principles were legitimized by the 1946 Full Employment Act. Not only did the Act charge government with the responsibility to adjust fiscal policy to insure full employment, it also created the Council of Economic Advisors to guarantee the president a staff of professional economists to insure he made the right decisions.

What advice could these economists offer the President? Keynes had already provided part of the answer by stressing the importance of fiscal policy (especially government spending) for stimulating the economy. But monetary policy would also play a role, though by 1952 control of monetary policy had shifted to the Federal Reserve Board with only nominal influence exercised by either Congress or the President.

Until recently, the principal goal of economic policy has been to use fiscal and monetary tools to stabilize prices (keep inflation low) and promote full employment. However, as we shall see, because of political pressures the government's ability to attempt anything bold with either fiscal or monetary policy has been severely limited.

Though stabilization has had top priority, new problems have cropped up. Today, increasing worker productivity and reducing the size of the federal deficit have been added to the agenda.

We will have a look at these two problems later. Right now we will concentrate on how government can use fiscal and monetary policy to control the problems of unemployment and inflation.

NOTES

[1]Irving Welfeld, Where We Live (New York: Simon and Schuster, 1988), p. 55.

[2]Ibid., p. 107.

[3] Landon Jones, *Great Expectations* (New York: Ballantine Books, 1980), p. 39.

[4]Paul Light, *Baby Boomers* (New York: W.W. Norton & Company, 1988), p. 119.

[5]Landon Jones, *Great Expectations*, p. 57.

[6]Godfrey Hodgson, *America in Our Time* (New York: Doubleday & Company,

1976), p. 29.

[7]David Halberstam, *The Reckoning* (New York: William Morrow and Company, 1986), p. 275.

[8]Ibid., ch. 17.

[9]Ibid., p. 717.

Chapter 5
Fiscal Policy

The tools of fiscal policy are taxes and spending. These two tools can be used to increase aggregate demand, providing a strong stimulus to the economy. When demand rises, sales of goods and services increase and employment expands. Aggregate demand can be raised by reducing taxes, or by increasing spending. We will examine tax reduction shortly. Right now we will concentrate on the effects of increased spending.

INCREASING AGGREGATE DEMAND

SPENDING

Increased government spending stimulates the economy by raising aggregate demand for goods and services. It doesn't matter what the spending is for. What is important is that people earn income from the spending so that they can turn around and purchase the normal things people buy.

For example, federal funds spent to maintain Fairchild Air Force Base in Spokane, Washington help stimulate the local economy. Fairchild is a huge complex with over seven million square feet of buildings spread out over 5,300 acres. The base has its own hospital and cable TV station. It has nearly six thousand personnel and provides housing for 1,580 officers and enlisted men. In addition to maintaining the 92d Heavy Bombardment Wing of B52s, Fairchild also manages a military survival school. The total value of its B52 bombers, KC-135 refueling tankers, air launched cruise missiles, helicopters and training aircraft exceeds $2 billion.

Fairchild is a direct source of jobs for 900 Spokane residents. In

1989, the base's civilian employees earned over $14 million. In that same year, construction and service contracts to local firms totaled more than $12 million. The total payroll for the base was more than $61 million. Much of that was spent in the local economy. Indeed, over 2,000 military personnel live off base in homes they are purchasing or in rented apartments. Military personnel purchase cars from Spokane dealerships, and shop in Spokane markets. With a yearly utility bill of nearly $6 million, local utility companies also benefit from the base's presence. So do local colleges. In 1989, 1,768 military personnel from the base were enrolled in college courses.

But that isn't the end of Fairchild's economic impact on Spokane. Many officers and enlisted men who see duty at Fairchild eventually choose to retire in Spokane, and add their retirement dollars to the local economy. In 1989, those dollars were considerable—over $88 million.

Not only does all this money increase sales in Spokane, it also generates more jobs in the civilian economy. Estimates are that, in 1989, the combined effect of military payroll, construction and service contracts to local firms plus the impact of retirement income resulted in 3,675 additional jobs in the Spokane area.[1] If Fairchild were closed, the economic impact on the Spokane businesses community would be considerable.

Business leaders in Spokane are aware of this fact. The Chamber of Commerce even has a special Military Affairs Committee to promote political support for Fairchild. Since Spokane's Congressman, Tom Foley, is Speaker of the House and one of the most powerful politicians in the country, community leaders remain confident the base will not be closed any time soon. However, fears that improved relations between the U.S. and the Soviet Union might result in major cuts in defense spending prompted Spokane businessmen to pay for a computer analysis of the possible economic effects of future cutbacks in Fairchild's budget. The study revealed that a $50 million (the worst case scenario) cut in spending would result in a loss of over a thousand jobs in Spokane,[2] highlighting the importance of Fairchild to the economic health of the local economy.

While government spending can do a great deal to stimulate the economy, in order for increased spending to have the desired effect, government must not try to pay for it through higher taxes. This would be self-defeating. Increased spending would put money in people's pockets while higher taxes would take it away. The one would increase, the other decrease, aggregate demand. So to be effective, taxes must not be raised to cover increases in spending. This means government will have to run a deficit, spending more money than it takes in through taxes.

TAX REDUCTION

Aggregate demand can also be elevated by a tax cut. Lowering taxes increases takehome pay for taxpayers. They can buy more than before. These extra purchases stimulate the economy. Again, to make this work there will have to be a budget deficit. After all, a tax cut means lower government revenues. Government dare not reduce spending to balance the budget. This would reduce demand, offsetting the increase in demand achieved by the tax cut.

FINANCING THE DEFICIT

By now it should be clear that budget deficits are an essential aspect of increasing demand either through increased spending or reduced taxes. Of course, if the economy is already growing rapidly on its own, or unemployment is low, there may be no need for government to stimulate the economy. However, if unemployment is high, or economic growth sluggish, there may be good reason for government to attempt to stimulate it. And if fiscal rather than monetary policy is to be used, this means running a deficit.

Since deficits are so central to Keynesian fiscal policy, it is worth asking how the federal government finances a deficit once it occurs.

One way is to create new money to pay for the deficit. This new money is created when the federal government sells securities (pledges for repayment) to the nation's central bank, the Federal Reserve Bank.

Suppose the sale is for $50 billion worth of securities. When the Federal Reserve receives the securities, it credits the $50 billion to the government's account. It just writes down that amount in a ledger, creating the new money. Now the federal government can legally write checks for an additional $50 billion. A problem with this method of financing the deficit is that it can be highly inflationary. With all that new money injected into the economy, more dollars (or checks) than before are chasing a fixed amount of goods. Prices naturally rise in reaction.

A second way to pay for the deficit is to borrow the necessary funds from private investors through a medium like Treasury Bills. These are sold on the open market to individuals and institutional investors like pension funds. The money used to purchase Treasury Bills is money already in circulation; and if the economy is in recession a good deal of the money is likely to come from savings accounts in banks—the leakages Keynes worried so much about. This kind of deficit financing helps soak up unused savings and gets it working in the economy again. And since it's not new money, it doesn't increase the money supply and therefore is not inflationary. Usually, deficits are financed mostly in this way.

REDUCING AGGREGATE DEMAND

REDUCED SPENDING

If increased spending, or lowered taxes, tends to stimulate the economy, the opposite fiscal policies tend to cause the economy to contract. A cutback in government spending contracts the economy by reducing incomes. For example, a reduction in welfare payments reduces the incomes of welfare families; a cut in defense spending reduces the incomes of defense firms and their employees. This drop in income leads to a decline in purchases. Because of the drop in demand some businesses begin to lay off workers and reduce orders to their suppliers. Eventually, less is being produced than before. This is an economic contraction.

INCREASED TAXES

A tax increase can also contract the economy. It all depends on what government does with the extra taxes. If it spends it all, then it may not cause the economy to contract because the money taken from taxpayers is spent by government. However, if the government runs a budget surplus, that is collects the money but doesn't spend it, then the economy will certainly contract because aggregate demand will be less than before.

Now that we have an idea how to stimulate or to cool down the economy, it shouldn't be difficult to see how fiscal policy can be used to reduce unemployment or fight inflation.

UNEMPLOYMENT

Generally, people are unemployed because the economy can get by without them. There is not enough demand for goods and services to warrant hiring more workers. The simple solution is to increase aggregate demand by increasing government spending or reducing taxes.

The favorite fiscal policy for reducing unemployment has been increased spending rather than a reduction of taxes. Part of the reason is politics. Congressmen can take credit for expenditures that benefit their constituents. They can't take as much credit for a tax cut that goes to everyone. Indeed, the pressure to reward constituents with direct benefits is so great that spending increases often occur for that reason alone, regardless of the level of unemployment.

But preferring spending over tax reduction to reduce unemployment also makes some economic sense. It has to do with another idea hatched by Keynes. It's called the multiplier effect. The idea is that money used to purchase things becomes someone's income which in turn is used to purchase more things, creating more income. The money turns into income and spending over and over again. Of course, some of it leaks out as savings (or taxes or investment in a pension fund), so the exact value of the multiplier depends on the prevailing marginal propensity to consume (MPC)—the amount of income spent rather than saved. There is a simple formula to calculate the multiplier when it is adjusted for the effect of how much income is spent rather than saved:

$$\text{Multiplier}=1/(1\text{-MPC})$$

Thus, if it was determined that people spent 75 percent of their income, the multiplier would be:

$$\text{Multiplier}=1/(1\text{-.75}), \quad \text{or} \quad 1/.25=4$$

This means that if government increased spending by $1 million, it would be multiplied four times, resulting in an addition of spending in the economy of $4 million. What if government tried to achieve the same thing by a tax cut? Would $1 million extra income be multiplied in the same way? If marginal propensity to consume (MPC) is .75, then we should expect that only $750,000 of the tax cut would be spent; the rest would be diverted to savings or some other purpose. We already know our multiplier is 4, so the total spending will be $750,000 X 4, or $3 million. Compared to the $4 million in purchasing power generated by government spending, that's a $1 million loss. So government spending is a more effective way of increasing aggregate demand.

On the other hand, most tax payers would probably prefer a tax cut to increased government spending to reduce unemployment, even if it costs more in the long run. At least they would be spending the money rather than the government. Despite this preference, government has favored spending rather than tax reduction to increase demand. True, since the end the Second World War, taxes have been repeatedly reduced, but only selectively. Corporations and wealthy individuals have been the prime beneficiaries of cuts in capital gains taxes, investment tax credits, or the reduction of tax liability through the accelerated depreciation of buildings and equipment. Only twice since 1945 have there been across the board cuts for all taxpayers. Why? As already indicated, the political process is partly responsible. Congressmen prefer spending to tax cuts. But another reason is that by the late 1960s when Keynesian economic policy had become orthodoxy, concerns about unemployment were fading into the background to be replaced by worries about mounting inflation. Unemployment wasn't the big issue and increasing aggregate demand through tax cuts did not attract as much interest as before.

INFLATION

While raising aggregate demand reduces unemployment, lowering it reduces inflation. This works because a decline in demand results in unsold inventories building up in stores and warehouses. It's not long before orders for new goods are curtailed. Eventually, factories have to layoff workers because there is not enough for them to do. This all has an effect on prices. Merchants have to cut prices to persuade shoppers to purchase unsold inventories. Factories have to lower their prices to get stores to order more goods. Unemployed workers can't buy as much as before, so merchants have to lower prices even further to clear out inventory.

So the key is to reduce demand. As we have already discovered, this can be achieved either by spending cuts or tax increases. A budget cut means there will be less money buying goods and services, and this decline in demand will force prices downward. An increase in taxes leaves workers with less takehome pay. They can't buy as much as before. If the economy responds correctly, prices will decline.

One problem with fighting inflation by decreasing demand is that it can cause unemployment. In theory, the amount of unemployment might not be very high if it is demand-pull inflation. Demand-pull inflation occurs when the economy is operating at full, or near full capacity, and demand for goods and services still outstrips the available supply.[3] In this situation, nearly everyone who wants to work is already employed, and factories are operating at full tilt. But because of the excess demand, it is impossible to fill all the orders streaming in from anxious merchants. Shortages occur, and won't go away until there is new investment to increase capacity. This takes time. Meanwhile scarce resources are rationed to the highest bidder. If government were to decrease demand so that it no longer exceeds but matches capacity, then inflation might decline without causing layoffs. Eliminating shortages simply relieves the pressure on prices. If this relief is provided while the economy is still operating at full capacity, businesses can't afford to layoff workers. At most, employers might cut back on the overtime that was needed to fill excess orders for goods. But no one will be fired because there will still be sufficient demand to keep all employees busy on their regular shifts. Consequently, in this situation, prices might decline without unemployment rising.

But what if inflation is caused by high production costs rather than too much demand, what economists call cost-push inflation? That was the problem in the 1970s. Labor became expensive, and energy prices rose to record levels. One reason for the high cost of labor was union contracts in major industries providing cost of living increases in addition to hikes in real wages. Millions of union workers saw their wages grow well beyond the national average. In addition, energy prices increased after the OPEC oil embargo of 1973 and eventually reached a record high in 1979. Faced with higher labor and energy costs, many firms simply passed the increased costs along to consumers in the form of higher prices for their products.

In such a situation, a sharp reduction in demand might wring cost-push inflation out of the economy, but only by causing severe unemployment. Because a large share of the inflation is the result of excessive costs and not excessive demand, a reduction in demand would result in unsold goods rather than, as with demand-push inflation, merely a decline in shortages. Unsold goods eventually mean layoffs to cut costs. Of course, cutting costs is the whole point. But increased unemployment is also a consequence.

Faced with this prospect, policy makers in the decade of the 1970s were reluctant to administer this bitter pill to the economy. The baby-boomers were entering the work force. To absorb them all required more than 2 million new jobs per year. The economy was growing but not that fast, so unemployment remained high throughout the decade. To assault inflation by attacking demand would have slowed job creation and raised unemployment figures even higher, likely into the double digit range. Neither Nixon, Ford nor Carter were willing to be responsible for that much pain.

It wasn't until the early 1980s, during the Reagan administration, that this attitude changed. It was not only that the new administration was more calloused about high unemployment, though this was a factor. There was also a recognition that curing inflation in the 1980s would not be as costly in terms of unemployment as it would have been in the 1970s. This is because the surge of new job seekers was beginning to peter out. Where it had taken about 2.1 million new jobs per year to absorb incoming baby-boomers in the 1970s, it required on average only 1.7 million new jobs in the 1980s to absorb most of them.[4]

Ironically, even though Reagan was willing to take on inflation, his fiscal policy aggravated instead of helped to reduce it. It was monetary policy orchestrated mostly by the Federal Reserve, though endorsed by Reagan, that eventually broke the back of runaway inflation.

NOTES

[1]*Fairchild Economic Resource Impact Statement (1989)*, prepared by 92d Cost Analysis Branch, pp. 10,13, 31, 35-47.

[2]Jim Camden, "'Low-end' scenario would drain Spokane," *Spokane Chronicle* (Aug 5, 1990).

[3]Actually, inflation generally occurs when the economy operates beyond 85 percent of capacity. Experience shows that beyond that point it becomes difficult for factories to operate efficiently.

[4]John Schwarz, *America's Hidden Success*, revised ed. (New York: W.W. Norton, 1988), p. 167.

Chapter 6
Monetary Policy

It is widely believed that the supply of money in an economy has a powerful effect on aggregate demand; an increase in the supply of money increases demand, a decrease reduces it. How does this occur? The simple theory is that when the money supply is increased, more dollars are available for consumption. This translates into an increase in demand for goods and services. On the other hand, when the money supply is reduced, less dollars are available for consumption. Less is purchased than before. This is a decline in demand. If the simple theory is correct, it means increasing the supply of money (increasing demand) should help reduce unemployment, and decreasing it (reducing demand) would be an important tool for fighting inflation.

Before examining this in more detail it is worth asking how the money supply gets changed. Actually, banks do it all the time in the course of their normal operations. Banks create money by making loans and purchasing securities and bonds. They reduce the money supply when they cut back on loans and sell securities and bonds.

CREATING MONEY

Let's give this a closer look. What counts as money? Today, most money comes in the form of checks and a much smaller amount in cash and coin. Checks and currency count as money because we accept them as such. They don't have much value apart from that. Nothing backs them up. The U.S. effectively went off the gold standard in 1933 when U.S. citizens could no longer exchange dollars for gold. However, after the Second World War, the U.S. government did agree to exchange gold for dollars with central banks of foreign nations at the set price of $35 per ounce. But by the late 1960s, the market price of gold was much higher than this amount and many foreign banks began exchanging surplus dollars in their accounts for U.S. gold, which they then sold on the free market for a higher price. By 1971, the drain of gold from the U.S. Treasury was so severe President Nixon agreed to suspend convertibility. Now, whether home or abroad, nothing backs the dollar but confidence in the U.S. economy.

Some people long for a return to the gold standard. They think it would make money more stable, less prone to inflation. That certainly wouldn't be the effect if the switch were sudden. Since 1973, the official U.S. price of gold has been $42.22 per ounce. At that price, the Federal reserve has gold worth about $11 billion. Of course, the market price of gold is around $400 per ounce, which means if we returned to the gold standard and allowed the market price of gold to determine the worth of the dollar, the Federal Reserve's gold supply would immediately be worth about $104 billion. The money supply would have suddenly increased dramatically, fueling inflation.[1]

It is true that a gold standard helps to stabilize the money supply since the amount of money depends on the total amount of gold available. Baring new discoveries of gold deposits, the growth in money would always remain small. But most economists view this as a defect rather than a virtue. At the very least the money supply needs to expand as fast as the growth in the economy. If it lags behind, as it surely will during a period of rapid growth, prices will fall because the supply of goods outruns the supply of money.

Declining prices is hardly an incentive for continued investment in the economy, and can easily bring growth to a rapid halt. It is also proof that a stable money supply does not guarantee stable prices. The money supply can remain relatively stable and yet the general level of prices rise and fall in response to changes in total output—which is exactly what occurred in America when it was on a gold standard. This very point was made by Keynes when he argued that only by abandoning the gold standard and allowing central banks to manipulate the money supply could price stability ever be achieved.

Perhaps the most serious objection to a gold standard by liberal economists who worry about unemployment as much as inflation is that it pretty much eliminates the option to reduce unemployment by raising demand through an increase in the money supply.

How Banks Do It

For most people, the abandonment of the gold standard is slight cause for concern. Currency is treated as real money, and people think nothing of writing checks to purchase goods, or accepting checks for their wages. Good thing, too, because checks and checking accounts are one of the things that make money creation possible.

Economists talk of different kinds of money, but the one they usually employ for calculating the money supply is called M1 money. It includes all the cash not in banks but in circulation, and all the money represented by checking accounts in the U.S. M1 money is highly liquid. It is likely it will be immediately used, or flow (hence the term liquid) through the economy. Cash in a savings account is not liquid in this sense. The depositor is unlikely to spend it all or even a portion of it for some time.

Suppose I have a savings account with the Lincoln Heights branch of the US Bank in Spokane, Washington, and deposit $10,000 in cash in my account—even professors can engage in wishful thinking. What I have done through my deposit is remove $10,000 from the M1 money supply. Remember, if money is in a savings account in a bank and therefore not circulating, it is not part of the M1 money. But don't worry, most of it will get back into circulation in a different form shortly.

Not only will my deposit be credited to my savings account, but it will also become an asset of US Bank. Some of my cash deposit will be set aside in the bank's vault, but most of it will be deposited with the Federal Reserve and credited to US Bank's account so it can write checks on its funds, including my money. In fact, US Bank can legally use up to 88 percent of my $10,000 deposit for loans or investments. That's because the Federal Reserve, which oversees America's banking system, sets the reserve requirement for US Bank and other banks which are members of the Federal Reserve system. The reserve requirement is simply the percent of money in savings and checking accounts banks have to set aside in a *reserve* before they can begin to use depositors' money to make loans. One reason for the reserve requirement is to insure banks have enough money on hand to pay depositors when they come in and draw out funds from their accounts. But a more important reason is to give the Federal Reserve some control over the volume of bank loans. The higher the reserve the smaller that volume, the lower the reserve requirement the greater will be the volume of loans. Presently (1990), the reserve requirement is 12 percent, which means that 88 percent of the sum of all deposits can be used for loans.

With a reserve requirement of 12 percent, my bank can loan out $8,800 of my deposit. Unless someone asks for cash, the loan will be paid to a borrower by check, essentially a bank IOU. And it is here that US bank creates new money. When I deposited the $10,000 in my savings account, the M1 money supply declined by that amount. When US Bank writes a check for an $8,800 loan, M1 money supply instantly grows by that amount. Still, there is $1,200 less M1 money than there was before I deposited my $10,000. But this deficit will quickly vanish and become a surplus.

As far as US Bank is concerned, it hasn't really created money out of thin air. It had assets sufficient to cover all transactions. It had $10,000 in assets from my deposit. It loaned $8,800 of that out. But the borrower signed a loan agreement to pay back the entire amount, and probably had to pledge some collateral as well. This loan agreement is an asset worth $8,800 and will appear as such on the bank's balance sheet. Thus, while the bank's $10,000 asset (my deposit) was reduced to $1,200 by loan, the $8,800 loan agreement is a new asset that balances out the loss. The bank still has the $10,000 but just in a different form.

Of course, the whole transaction was made possible by my deposit which the bank used as an asset for the loan, and on which it charges interest—a lucrative source of income for the bank. An eminent lawyer and advisor to Presidents, George Ball, who entered banking late in life was reported to have exclaimed, once he understood the process just described, "Why didn't someone tell me about banking before?"[2]

To return to the $8,800 loan, eventually the money will become purchases. And here is where money creation really takes off. Since most of the money for these purchases will be deposited in checking accounts of the businesses where the purchases were made, this money will remain part of M1. Remember, M1 includes cash outside of banks plus all the money in checking accounts. While the cash I deposited in my savings account reduced M1, a deposit in a checking account does not. The deposited amount remains part of M1. Thus, the money supply was permanently increased by the loan.

But that isn't the end of the story. Since the money in these checking accounts qualifies as new bank assets, it can justify additional loans. Again, the new loans will eventually wind up as deposits in other checking accounts from which new loans will be made. Of course, because of the 12 percent reserve requirement, each new round of loans generates less new money than the previous round. When the original loan of $8,800 becomes a deposit, only $7,744 of it can be used for loans. When this becomes deposits, only $6,814.72 can be loaned out, etc.

TABLE 2

Money Creation (12% Reserve Requirement)

Bank	New Deposit	Loaned Out
1	$10,000.00	$8,800.00
2	$8,800.00	$7,744.00
3	$7,744.00	$6,814.72
4	$6,814.72	$5,996.95
:	:	:
114	$0	$0
New Money	➡	$73,333.30

Theoretically, the process of creating money through new rounds of loans can continue until the last deposit approaches zero. In the case of my $10,000, the loans would have to be recycled about 114 times. As you can see from Table 2, the total amount of new money created would amount to $73,333.30. That's an increase over the original $8,800 loan by a factor of 8.3.

There is an easier way to calculate the maximum possible expansion of deposited money than working it out on paper, or even using a spreadsheet if you own a computer. A simple formula does all the work for you.

$$Expansion=(1/reserve)$$

At a reserve requirement of 12 percent, this becomes

$$Expansion=1/0.12, \quad or \quad 8.33$$

The original $8,800 loan multiplied by 8.33 equals $73,304, pretty close to the total in Table 2.

In reality, the expansion is never that large. One reason is that money doesn't turn over as often as pure theory allows. Another reason is that banks are sometimes cautious and don't loan out everything over the reserve requirement. The more cautious they are, the smaller the money expansion. A third reason the expansion is not as great as it might be in theory is that loans are constantly being paid off, and this contracts the money supply. Loans are usually repaid with checks, the amount being subtracted from the payer's checking account, reducing the deposit amount available for making new loans. So the expansion of the total money supply from loans may actually be quite modest, perhaps five to eight percentage points per year in good times. That is unless the Federal Reserve intervenes.

At the start, we mentioned another way banks can create new money and expand the money supply. They do it by purchasing bonds and securities. They don't use their own money, of course. Instead they use the assets represented by deposited money, or at least the amount left after subtracting the reserve requirement. So bank checks for bonds and securities becomes new money, which is deposited into bank accounts and can be used to make loans or to purchase more bonds and securities.

HOW THE FED CONTROLS THE MONEY SUPPLY

The Federal Reserve can help banks create more money in several ways. First, it can lower the reserve requirement for member banks, permitting them to loan out a larger portion of deposits than before. In the example above, if the reserve were only 10 instead of 12 percent, the maximum expansion would be 10 rather than 8.33, and the total increase in new money from my $10,000 deposit would be $90,000 (10 x $9,000) instead of $73,304.

The Federal Reserve can also increase the amount of money banks have available for loans by offering attractive loans to member banks. This is done by lowering the discount rate, the interest rate the Fed (the nickname economists and bankers use for the Federal Reserve) charges member banks for loans, down to the point where it is too attractive to pass up. Suppose the prevailing interest rate on loans, the rate banks charge their own borrowers, was 11 percent. Now the Fed offers these banks money at nine percent. That's a two percent difference. Banks can borrow Fed funds at this lower rate and loan it out at the higher rate, pocketing the difference. Normally, banks will greedily take the bait, and in the process loan out more money and expand the money supply.

The Fed can achieve the same result by purchasing government bonds or securities from banks. A special section of the Fed does nothing but buy and sell bonds to banks. It's called the Open Market Committee. To get banks to sell bonds, the Open Market Committee offers to buy bonds at an attractive rate, usually a fraction above the prevailing market rate. Banks unload their bonds for cash (or more accurately checks written by the Fed) and realize they have more money available to loan out. With all the extra money to loan out, in no time the money supply expands. The Fed generally relies on the Open Market Committee more than anything else to expand and, as we shall see, to contract the money supply.

The Fed can also contract the money supply. First, it can raise the reserve requirement so a smaller portion of existing bank deposits can become loans. In time, as the amount of new money being created declines, and old loans are paid off, the money supply begins to contract.

The Fed can raise the discount rate, making it less attractive for member banks to borrow additional money from the Fed for new loans; this may not actually contract the money supply, but it certainly will close off this avenue of additional expansion.

And, third, the Fed can sell bonds and securities to banks, siphoning money out of the banking system into its own account where it can sit on it. Again, there will be less money in banks available for loans; the money supply will contract.

UNEMPLOYMENT AND INFLATION

It is now easy to see how monetary policy can be used to reduce unemployment or to fight inflation. By using its powers to increase the money supply—lower reserve requirement, purchase bonds, lower discount rate—the Fed can pump more money into the economy, stimulating demand for goods and services which, in turn, will eventually increase demand for new workers and reduce unemployment. Unfortunately, if the increase in the money supply is large and occurs suddenly, it can set off a wave of inflation. Historically, the Fed has been more concerned with curbing inflation than reducing unemployment. Only occasionally, when pressured by the President, has it set aside this prejudice and chanced inflation by rapidly expanding the supply of money.

Inflation can be curbed by contracting the money supply. Raising the reserve requirement, selling bonds, or increasing the discount rate are all tools the Fed can used to bring this about. With fewer dollars chasing the same amount of goods, prices have to drop to clear inventories. As we shall see, small contractions of the money supply don't seem to work very well when inflation has persisted for some time. Indeed, it took a

dramatic and sharp contraction of the money supply to end the inflation of
the 1970s. It also caused a severe recession, the worst since the Great
Depression.

TABLE 3

Fiscal Policy

Increase Employment Increase Inflation		Reduce Employment Reduce Inflation
Lower	⇐ Taxes ⇒	Raise
Increase	⇐ Spending ⇒	Reduce

Monetary Policy

Increase Employment Increase Inflation		Reduce Employment Reduce Inflation
$+ Lower	⇐ Reserve Req. ⇒	Increase $-
$+ Lower	⇐ Discount Rate⇒	Increase $-
$+ Buy	⇐ Bonds ⇒	Sell $-

To summarize, government can use either fiscal or monetary policy
(or both in tandem) to fight unemployment or inflation. Lower taxes or
increased spending reduces unemployment, as does an increase in the

money supply. Increased taxes or decreased spending fights inflation, as does a reduction in the money supply.

The various techniques of fiscal and monetary policy and their outcomes are represented in Table 3.

NOTES

[1] Sidney Weintraub, *Our Stagflation Malaise* (Westport, Connecticut: Quorum Books, 1981), p. 69.

[2] quoted in John K. Galbraith, *Money:Whence It Came, Where It Went*, p. 20.

Chapter 7
Actual Policy

By the end of the Second World War, Keynesian economics had become orthodoxy, at least among most economists. And the 1946 Full Employment Act established fiscal policy as an important tool for maintaining full employment. Nevertheless, members of the President's new Council of Economic Advisors were not given a free hand to shape fiscal (or monetary) policy to achieve the Keynesian goal of full employment and stable prices.

The simple reason for this imposed restraint was hostility from the business community. Many businessmen remained unconvinced government should play as large a role in directing the economy as Keynes had recommended. For one thing, it implied that businessmen in their daily struggle to make a profit were mostly irrelevant to the health of the economy. Instead, what mattered was government's ability to raise or lower taxes, increase or decrease government spending, and control the money supply to stimulate or depress aggregate demand. In fact, this was pretty much what Keynes himself believed. Indeed, he presumed that if left to themselves businessmen were more likely to make a mess of things rather than promote economic health.

STABILIZERS

Naturally, business leaders didn't warm to this idea. They believed they still had an important role to play. Moreover, they were ideologically opposed to government management of the economy. Public opinion, however, was on the side of more, not less government supervision of the economy. So business spokesmen sought a compromise, giving government a role but one less activist than many Keynesians desired.[1] The compromise was that government would use various stabilizers to automatically control unemployment and inflation. In fact, most of these stabilizers were already in place. There was the budget itself which, if held relatively constant could exercise a stabilizing effect. Then there was the progressive income tax which by then covered most wage earners in America. There was Social Security and Unemployment Compensation and Aid to Families with Dependent Children.

How could these programs function as stabilizers? Well, for one thing, Social Security and AFDC guaranteed that a large number of Americans received incomes even when the economy turned sour. And unemployment compensation insured laid-off workers some income during a recession. Today these are called safety nets. For the average citizen their prime purpose is to prevent the elderly or disadvantaged or unemployed from suffering grinding poverty. Compassion is their justification. But for the economist these programs also insure that a significant number of people will have incomes regardless of the state of the economy. This is an important tool for battling recessions caused by declining aggregate demand. Social Security payments, unemployment checks, and welfare subsidies become income for millions, most of whom will spend it all for goods and services, propping up sagging aggregate demand.

The size of government is another stabilizer. Few federal employees are laid off during a recession, so their purchasing power remains more or less constant, helping to prop up the economy during bad times. Today, this prop is substantial. The federal government employs around 3 million workers—5 million if military personnel are included. State and local governments add another 13 million employees. These 18 million employees constitute about 17 percent of the workforce.[2] Millions more earn their living by working for firms who contract with the government, bringing the number of employees either directly or indirectly employed by government (federal, state, and local) to about 25 percent of the entire workforce. So much constant purchasing power exercises considerable stabilizing force on the economy and generally prevents recessions from becoming too severe.

A major assumption in the stabilization scheme was that the level of government spending, the size of the budget, would remain constant during a recession. There would be no budget cuts. This meant tolerating deficits in bad times because during recessions tax receipts fall and revenue declines. Not enough is taken in to cover expenses. But by keeping spending constant and tolerating a deficit, the recession would never be too severe. This is because government purchases would remain about the same, functioning as a steady source of high aggregate demand. Eventually the economy would turn around, economic growth would pick up, and revenues would increase. The deficit would soon disappear and the budget would be balanced.

There were also built-in stabilizers to dampen inflation when it occurred. The progressive income tax was viewed as the principal safeguard here. For example, if the economy grew too fast and inflation (both in prices and wages) began to spread, the income tax would automatically adjust to the change and help to cool things down by reducing aggregate demand. This would happen because of the progressivity of the tax. The higher one's income, the higher the proportion of it taken away in taxes. Inflated wages would shove workers into higher tax brackets and increase the amount of taxes they had to pay. Tax revenues would increase rapidly. This additional revenue would not be spent, however. For, as with recessions, the size of the budget would remain constant. There would be no increases, no cuts. But in the case of inflation it wouldn't mean running a deficit but instead building up a surplus. There would be more revenue coming in than required to cover expenses. This surplus is money withdrawn from the economy, money that could not be used for purchases. Aggregate demand would naturally decline as a result, cooling down the economy. Soon economic growth would moderate, prices and wages would decline, and tax revenues would sooner or later fall. With declining tax revenues the budget surplus would disappear and everything would be back to normal. All of this would occur automatically, without politicians raising or lowering taxes, increasing or decreasing spending.

The business community warmed to the idea of using these stabilizers, relying on a stable budget and relatively stable transfer payments to the unemployed and Social Security and welfare recipients to maintain a stable economy. They preferred this arrangement to free-wheeling Keynesianism because it restricted political tinkering with the economy. Since it was believed a constant budget served to stabilize the economy during either recession or rising inflation, it was argued that there was no economic justification for dramatic increases in government spending. The other stabilizers like Social Security, welfare, and unemployment compensation served a similar role. Once in place, there was no legitimate economic reason for increasing their size or adding new programs to the list. In sum, politicians would not have an excuse for massive spending, nor a legitimate economic reason for expanding welfare. As far as businessmen were concerned, the compromise was a wonderful way to make Keynesian economic policy serve conservative economic goals.

DEFENSE SPENDING

The use of stabilizers for guiding fiscal policy dominated economic policy until the early 1960s. This does not mean there were not important changes. But they did not alter the basic arrangement. The most important change was the size and permanency of defense spending due to emergence of the Cold War. Defense spending grew dramatically during the Korean war, reaching 13 percent of GNP in 1953. Yet even after the Korean war spending remained high. In fact, with the exception of the Vietnam War and the Reagan years, defense spending in constant dollars (dollars adjusted for inflation) has remained relatively constant, give or take $10 or $20 billion (see Figure 1).[3]

FIGURE 1

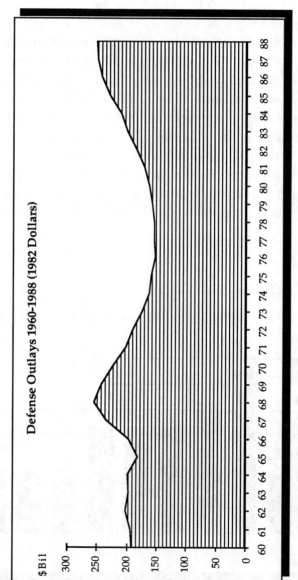

Defense Outlays 1960-1988 (1982 Dollars)

Source: *Statistical; Abstract of the United States* (1990), p.330.

IDEOLOGY AND POLITICS

One reason for the constancy of America's defense expenditures was the continued intensity of the ideological conflict between the U.S. and world communism. But another was the growth of what President Eisenhower called the "Military Industrial Complex". The complex he referred to was the growing industrial and high-tech sector of the American economy that had come to depend on federal defense contracts as its primary source of income. What Eisenhower feared was the political influence of these industries. He believed congressmen from districts with defense industries were prone to treat defense expenditures more as pork than defense, more as a way to funnel federal money to their constituents than to meet the needs of national defense. And he was right.

FIGURE 2

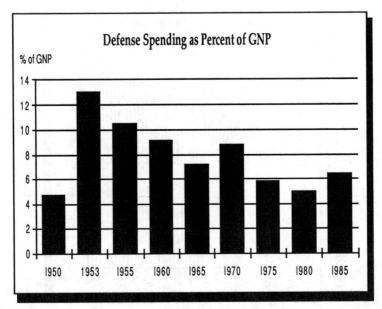

Source: *Statistical Abstract of the United States* (1979, 1990)

As a glance at Figure 2 reveals, defense spending has remained high through the decades, never dropping below 5 percent of GNP. At first, conservatives supported high levels of defense spending for ideological reasons, liberals for economic ones. Conservatives who might be expected to come out against excessive government spending seldom criticized such high levels of spending for defense. Indeed, they often argued for even higher amounts. This was not on economic grounds, for most rejected Keynesian spending as the road to economic health. Rather, they were in favor of a strong and aggressive national defense, and willing to tolerate huge budget deficits if necessary to achieve it. On the other hand, while many liberals were less hawkish about defense they nevertheless realized it was the one area of spending conservatives would tolerate, and one where the amount of money involved was so great it could have an enormous impact on aggregate demand and therefore on employment. And liberals have generally favored a full-employment economy.

Eventually, even conservative politicians came around to the economic view. Not because they converted to Keynesian economics, but because many of them had defense industries in their district. For it did not take long for the Department of Defense to learn it could gain political support for its budget items by awarding defense contracts to firms located in districts of powerful congressmen.

A recent example illustrates this much used tactic. Continued congressional support of Reagan's expensive Strategic Defense Initiative, popularly known as Star Wars, was greatly enhanced by the way research contracts were awarded. Star Wars was mostly a research program to develop laser weapons with great accuracy and power to destroy incoming nuclear missiles. No one was sure it could even be done, and the estimated price tag was somewhere around $800 billion,[4] with no promise that a feasible working model would be available anytime in the near future. Nevertheless, Congress supported the research, in part no doubt because the Defense Department awarded research contracts to forty-two of the fifty states, and in nearly every state of the members of the Senate Armed Services Committee. As one former presidential advisor observed, Star

Wars was being transformed "from stardust and moonbeams to that great pork barrel in the sky."[5]

NOT ALWAYS A GOOD THING

By the mid-1960s there was a general consensus among both conservatives and liberals that large defense outlays were good for the economy. However, there is good reason to doubt defense spending always exercises the salutary effect. Critics like the economist Seymour Melman have pointed out for years that large defense budgets in fact cripple the economy. For one thing, they divert enormous resources into non-productive spending. Very little of the technology developed for weapons winds up improving domestic products. Based on estimates from the Commerce Department, Melman argues that only about five percent of the technology in defense ever gets transferred to civilian technology.[6] Then there is the waste and inefficiency of defense production. Contracts are not always awarded on a pure competitive basis. As often as not, influence rather than competence wins contracts, which is why the top defense contractors tend to have the largest number of retired military officers on their payroll.[7] This gives them easy access to the Defense Department. Moreover, most defense contracts are on a cost plus basis, meaning firms charge whatever it costs them to manufacture a product plus an additional amount to guarantee a profit. There is little incentive to minimize costs. Rather, the incentive is to maximize them. Understandably, the efficiency of labor is low, often less than 50 percent when compared to comparable non-defense firms. This makes converting to domestic production difficult if not impossible for defense contractors. They have simply forgotten how to cut costs and compete. The few defense firms that have attempted the conversion have failed miserably.

Perhaps it is inevitable that weapons production will always be inefficient. For even if one were to factor out the inefficiency of labor in defense industries, the fact remains that defense firms are usually asked to produce new and untried weapon systems. It is only after much research and development and many false starts that the real cost of the final product can be accurately estimated.   Invariably, the final price tag is much higher than original estimates.   Possibly greater competition would reduce costs, force firms to be more efficient than they usually are; but this is often not possible.   The cost of weapons is already so high it would be prohibitively expensive to assign several competing firms the task of researching and manufacturing a weapon to discover which firm can do it for the least cost.

Nevertheless, even if inefficiency may be an inevitable fact of life of defense production, it unfortunately has consequences for non-defense industries.   In the past, the American economy outpaced its world competitors because of its lead in new technology which translated into innovative products and labor saving machinery increasing labor's productivity.[8] But beginning in the 1960s we began to fall behind in the race to develop new technology.   Indeed, between 1960 and 1982, the U.S. increased its imports of high technology products by over 1,000 percent.[9] Quality engineering has declined in the U.S., and our competitors have taken up the slack.   For example,

> in industry after industry requiring quality engineering there has been
> a manifest falling off of the U.S. position. Miniature ball bearings
> are an important component of many precision devices; by 1971 over
> half of the U.S. requirements of miniature ball bearings was supplied
> by imports, mainly from Japan.[10]

The U.S. has also fallen behind in the development of new technology to improve the productivity of workers.   As a consequence, productivity in the manufacturing sector has steadily declined.   Between 1948 and 1955 productivity in manufacturing increased at an annual rate of 3.2 percent.   This dropped to 2.8 percent between 1955 and 1965; it declined to 2.4 percent between 1965 and 1973, and dropped down to a mere 1.5 percent between 1973 and 1978.[11]

Seymour Melman and others point a finger at the defense industry as a major culprit in America's failure to remain in the lead in new technology, and for the steady decline in manufacturing productivity. They claim America has squandered funds for military research and spent little on the development of technology for the civilian sector of the economy. For example, between 1975 and 1988, about 2.5 percent of GNP went into research and development in the U.S. However, a large share of that money was diverted to defense research—27 percent in 1975 raised to 34.6 percent in 1988. For that same period, West Germany annually diverted only about 5 percent of total research spending to defense, and Japan nearly nothing at all. The lion's share of research funds in these major competitors for world markets went to research and development in the civilian sector where it counts economically.[12]

It is not only that Japan and West Germany spend a larger proportion of their GNP on civilian research and development than the U.S., it is also that research in the civilian sector is cheaper for them than for us. This is because our greater spending for defense research distorts the market. Trimming costs is not a high priority for defense firms, especially when it comes to hiring the best research talent. They pay top dollar for the best minds. This inflates the salaries of the engineers, scientists and mathematicians in the research field and raises the cost of research for the civilian sector. To get top engineers for a project, a non-defense company has to offer salaries high enough to compete with the prevailing wage rate in defense. When they do so, research costs are extremely high, much higher than in countries like Japan and West Germany. Often this proves too expensive and either the company has to cut back on research or settle for inexperienced or less talented researchers to do the job. Mostly, they have cut back.

Generally, criticism of large defense budgets has fallen on deaf ears. The public views them as the source of much needed jobs. So do the politicians they elect. In any case, since the early 1950s it has remained one of the principal props for economic stabilization, part of the policy status quo.

KENNEDY TAX CUT

However, the status quo of managing the economy through stabilizers was challenged by the Kennedy administration in the early 1960s. President Kennedy worried about the U.S. falling behind the Soviets in defense and in economic growth. His advisors, dedicated Keynesians all, suggested something bold. Why not lower taxes? This would stimulate aggregate demand and generate economic growth. Eventually, this growth would translate into more employed workers and higher real incomes. Taxes would still be lower, but there would be more taxpayers than before, and with better wages many would be in higher tax brackets. At some point, total tax revenue would actually become larger than before the tax cut.

Kennedy proposed the tax cut at the end of 1962. The proposal reduced taxes across the board and lowered the top tax rate from 91 to 70 percent, reducing the total tax load by about two percent of GNP. President Kennedy was assassinated before the tax reform worked its way through Congress where it was encountering difficulties because the government was already running about a $10 billion deficit which would be doubled by the proposed tax cuts. Partly because of respect for the slain President who had proposed the plan, the tax reduction proposal became law in early 1964 under Lyndon Johnson's administration.

The results of the tax cut were almost immediate. For several years the economy enjoyed rapid growth—7.1 percent in 1964, 8.1 percent in 1965, and 9.5 percent in 1966. And, as predicted, even at the lower rate the government's tax revenues began to climb until they outpaced expenditures. For the first time in years, the budget was in surplus. For many economists it was the first serious demonstration since the end of the Second World War of the complete validity of Keynesian economics.

THE GREAT SOCIETY

The budget surplus troubled many politicians. If it was allowed to persist it might eventually draw so much purchasing power out of the economy it could halt economic growth. President Johnson had a solution—the Great Society. It was his vision of greatly expanded welfare and civil rights legislation to put an end to both poverty and race discrimination in America. The civil rights legislation wouldn't cost much, but the welfare portion of his program would be very costly. Under normal circumstances, resistance to the Great Society would have been intense. Conservative Republicans along with conservative Southern Democrats had enough votes to stop it if they wished. Ideologically, they were opposed, and normally they would have objected to the expense. But Johnson could point to the budget surplus. It would cover the increase in spending. There would be no need for new taxes. The conservatives went along, and the largest expansion in welfare since the New Deal became law.

Social security benefits were increased, as was the AFDC component of Social Security. And, in 1965, two new programs were added. One was Medicare: government subsidized medical care for people over sixty-five. The other was Medicaid: medical subsidies for the poor. The Office of Economic Opportunity was created to provide job training to the poor. There was the Omnibus Housing Act to generate rent subsidies for low income citizens. Schools were given $1.3 billion in aid through the Elementary and Secondary Education Act. This was followed by the Higher Education Act which provided federal funds for college and university scholarships. And, finally, a Model Cities program was created to provide grants to clean up the nation's slums.

While there was enough revenue to cover all of this at the time, no one anticipated how large the system would grow over the years. By 1980, funds for these social programs had increased by 310 percent, dominating nearly half of the entire federal budget. Not that there weren't critics of welfare. But the problem they faced was that there was always enough money to pay for the programs, and that didn't make them look so expensive. The reason there was plenty of money is that shortly after welfare was expanded inflation began to plague the economy. As wages rose with prices, tax payers were shoved into higher tax brackets. Tax revenues grew accordingly, always providing enough money to pay for the programs as they expanded.

INFLATION

Spending on the Great Society might have been even greater if it hadn't been for the Vietnam war. The U.S. had become involved in Vietnam long before Johnson became president. Between 1950 and 1954, we gave France $3 billion to pay for the troops and military hardware needed to crush Vietnamese nationalism and preserve French colonialism in Southeast Asia. The French failed, and Vietnam was divided into two states—North Vietnam controlled by communist nationalists, and an anticommunist regime in South Vietnam sponsored by the U.S. From 1954 until 1965, the U.S. subsidized the South Vietnamese regime, and provided military assistance and training for its military forces. By 1964, it became clear that the South Vietnamese army could not defeat the communist guerrillas operating in the south, and the decision was made to turn the war into an all-American operation. In 1965, U.S. troop strength was increased from a few thousand to 200,000. By late 1967, there were more than 500,000 American soldiers in Vietnam.

AN EXPENSIVE WAR

But the large number of U.S. troops committed to the war tells only part of the story. True, it was a big war, though the French had as many soldiers in the field and still lost. The difference now was that in addition to a high troop commitment the Americans also factored in advanced technology. The conflict was transformed into a war of attrition, with the U.S. utilizing high technology weapons and logistics to destroy guerrillas and later regular North Vietnamese army forces. The idea was to employ economic and technological superiority to wear down the enemy, kill so many with superior fire power that the Vietnamese communists would eventually give up. The communists never did give up even though they suffered high loses. Thirteen Vietnamese soldiers were killed for every American soldier who died in battle. In all, between 600,000 and 1 million enemy soldiers were killed, about three percent of

Vietnam's entire population. For comparison, in World War Two, Japanese battle deaths amounted to only 1.4 percent of their population.[13]

American high technology allowed troops to be moved quickly over long distances with helicopters to engage the enemy. Foot soldiers were provided massive and devastating air support for operations against Viet Cong and North Vietnamese Army forces. And strategic bombing was employed on an unprecedented scale, not only in support of men in the field but to attack the enemy's supply lines and to strike strategic military, and later population, targets in the north. Six million tons of bombs were dropped on the Vietnamese, almost triple the tonnage of American bombs used in the Second World War.[14]

The high technology approach turned it into a very expensive war. The final price tag was about $140 billion, making it the second most costly war in U.S. history.[15]

In an effort to maintain popular support for the war, Johnson tried to prevent its huge price tag from becoming public knowledge. Higher taxes would certainly have alerted voters to the true cost of the war. So Johnson refused to raise taxes to cover the war's rising cost, at least until it was too late to make much of a difference. Budget deficits mounted, and the government had to borrow to make up the difference.

MONETIZING THE DEBT

As you may recall, there are two ways to pay for a deficit. The government can borrow from the private sector by selling bonds, or it can borrow from the Fed. The first way takes existing money available for investment and uses it for government purchases. No new money is created, and it doesn't cause inflation. The second way expands the money supply. The Fed simply writes the government a check, creating new money. This can cause inflation.

Johnson decided to mostly finance the deficit the second way by having the Fed create new money to cover the excess spending. He feared heavy government borrowing from the private sector would crowd out funds for private investment and slow down economic growth. This might lead to unemployment, and Johnson wanted to avoid that at all costs. So instead, he decided to monetize the debt. Between 1965 and 1970, federal debt rose by about $68 billion. Only $9 billion was borrowed from the private sector. The rest (about 50 percent of the total) came from the Fed in the form of new money, or was paid out of the receipts of various government trust funds, like Social Security.[16]

INFLATION BEGINS

The increase in the supply of money jumped from 4.5 percent in 1966 to to 9.2 percent in 1967.[17] With all that extra money injected into the economy, inflation naturally followed. From 1965 to 1968, the inflation rate increased from 1.7 to 4.2 percent. Johnson was finally persuaded by his economic advisors to slow down the increase in the money supply by dealing with its principal cause—the budget deficit. In the summer of 1968, Congress agreed to a ten percent surcharge on personal and corporate income taxes. In 1969 the deficit disappeared, yet the inflation rate continued to rise until it reached 5.9 percent in 1970.

A 5.9 percent inflation rate may seem small today, but that is because we experienced double digit inflation in the late 1970s and welcomed four and five percent inflation figures in the 1980s as a victory over inflation. But inflation was low in the 1950s and early 1960s, averaging about 1.5 percent for the period, and only 1.2 percent between 1960 and 1964. This made the 1970 inflation rate nearly 400 percent above the historical trend.

NIXON AND CONTROLS

When Nixon was elected in 1968, he promised to end the Vietnam War and to roll back inflation. It took him nearly five years to extricate us from Vietnam. Inflation never did go away.

Spending for the Vietnam war remained high during Nixon's first term, and the budget was again in deficit. This did not help the inflation picture. Also, Nixon was unwilling to solve the inflation problem by increasing unemployment. He believed this would hurt the Republicans at the polls. In fact, unemployment increased on its own in 1970 and 1971 despite high government spending. So Nixon rejected a tax increase or reduced spending as solutions for inflation. Either move would have probably made unemployment even worse.

Finally, in 1971, Nixon agreed to institute wage and price controls to reduce inflation. Actually, business was in favor of controls because unions were demanding big pay increases so wages could keep up with the rising inflation. Controls would get business off the hook.[18] Workers would have to accept a freeze on wages, and would be forced to blame government rather than their employer.

The controls started out as a strict freeze on prices and wages in major industries, were later moderated to allow for some leeway (about 5 percent) in price and wage increases, and eventually loosened further to allow for many exceptions. Even so, the controls helped some. Inflation declined in 1971 and 1972. But it rose to 6.2 percent 1973 mostly because of external force over which Nixon had no control.

INFLATION ABROAD

One of these forces was international banking. In 1944, it was agreed at a meeting of major trading nations at Bretton Woods in New Hampshire that the dollar would serve as the standard currency for international transactions after the War. All other currencies would have a fixed exchange rate with the dollar. For instance, the British pound was to be worth $2.80 and 360 Japanese yen were worth $1. If any of the signatories of the Bretton Woods agreement wanted to alter its currency's exchange rate with the dollar, it had to get the other members to agree. Also, the central banks of member nations were obliged to buy or sell dollars whenever necessary to maintain the stipulated exchange rates. For example, if the value of the dollar appeared to be declining vis-a-vis the yen, then the central banks were to buy dollars and unload yen. The increase in demand for the dollar would raise its worth, and the sale of yen (a drop in demand) would devalue Japan's currency. This buying and selling would continue until traders in the international money market adjusted their own purchases of dollars and yen to reflect the stipulated exchange rate. Once this was reached the central banks would exit the market.

The system worked remarkably well until 1971 when for the first time since the end of the Second World War the U.S. ran a trade deficit. It bought more from foreign nations than it sold to them. In particular, America imported more autos, steel and oil than it sold abroad. The U.S. had once dominated the world market for these products, but no more. We were losing our competitive edge in steel and autos, and simply running out of oil. Because we were purchasing so much from abroad dollars began to drain out of the U.S., piling up in foreign banks. Being in excess supply, the value of the dollar declined in international money markets. International money traders began unloading dollars for Japanese yen and German marks.

For two years until mid-1973, the central banks of the Bretton Woods signatories tried to shore up the value of the dollar by purchasing it on the open market, just as the Bretton Woods agreement required. The problem was that they did so by creating more of their own currency (writing checks from the account of the central bank) to cover the cost. This resulted in a rapid growth in the money supply in Japan and many European economies, causing inflation averaging about 12 percent per year in seven of the largest capitalist economies of the world.[19] This inflation seeped into the U.S. economy via higher priced imports from Europe and Japan. Inflation rose in the U.S.

In late 1973, the Bretton Woods agreement was more or less abandoned and the dollar allowed to seek its own level in the international market. Its exchange rate was immediately adjusted downward against most currencies. Unfortunately, this further increased the price of foreign goods, because it now took more dollars than before to purchase imports nominated in, say, marks or yen. Inflation in the U.S. worsened.

Ideologically Nixon was for free markets, and hated wage and price controls. He agreed to them only out of desperation. By 1973 they no longer seemed to be working. Not only had inflation increased anyway, but some producers refused to sell their products at the regulated price. Cattle were being held back from the market in anticipation that the controls would eventually be lifted; for the same reason chickens were being drowned rather than butchered and sold. And consumers anticipating the controls wouldn't last forever and prices would again skyrocket began a buying frenzy to stock up on goods sold at regulated prices. The controls were causing a shortage of goods and creating pressures for raising their prices. This was not eliminating inflation, it was stimulating forces that would eventually increase it. Clearly, the controls were beginning to distort the economy. In 1974, Nixon abandoned them.

BAD CROPS

By this time other forces were at work generating even more inflation. There were serious crop failures in the Soviet Union in 1972 and 1973. Wheat sales to Russia increased dramatically, causing shortages at home and eventually increased prices. The catch of anchovies of the coast of Peru declined precipitously during the same period. Anchovies were used extensively in animal feed, so the cost of raising poultry and other livestock jumped. Between 1972 and 1974, food costs in the U.S. rose by a whopping 34 percent.[20]

OIL

Then there was oil. Before mid-October 1973 the price of oil on the world market was $2.59 per barrel. After that date the price jumped to $11.65 a barrel, a 350 percent increase. The price increase was engineered by the Organization of Petroleum Exporting Countries (OPEC). Members of OPEC were mostly middle eastern oil kingdoms like Saudi Arabia, Kuwait, United Arab Emirates, Qatar, Iraq and Iran. But four African states also held membership—Libya, Algeria, Nigeria and Gabon. Indonesia was the only member from from Southeast Asia. And two members were Latin American countries—Venezuela and Ecuador. Saudi

Arabia, however, was the acknowledged leader of the organization.

Since OPEC's founding in 1961, the primary goal was to acquire more control over the price of crude oil. But prior to 1973, OPEC had been unable to break the power of the large international oil companies, known as the seven sisters—Exxon, Mobil, Standard Oil of California, Texaco, Gulf, Royal Dutch Shell, and British Petroleum. OPEC's only weapon in negotiating price increases was to threaten reductions in the amount of oil delivered to the big oil companies. Invariably this proved ineffective because of collusion between the seven sisters. If one of them faced reductions, the others shared their oil to make up the shortfall.

In 1967, after the crushing defeat of Egypt, Syria and Jordan by Israel in what came to be known as the six day war, some Arab members of OPEC tried to punish the U.S. for its support of Israel during the war by drastically cutting production. Saudi Arabia actually ceased production altogether for an entire month. However, the world price of oil did not rise, and the Arab states simply lost oil revenue. Nor was the U.S. hurt by the cutbacks. At that time the U.S. imported only 16 percent of the oil it consumed and only 2 percent came from the Arab oil states.[21] The boycott was barely noticed.

Two events altered this situation. One was domestic oil production in the U.S. The other was the ability of Libya to gain price concessions from the oil companies.

In 1970, production of oil in the U.S. began to decline. America was running out of oil. At the same time, demand for oil continued to rise. The only way to make up the difference was to import foreign oil. In that same year America imported 28 percent of the oil it used. It was now dependent on foreign markets.

A year earlier, in 1969, a young Libyan army officer, Muammar Qaddafi, led a successful coup and assumed leadership of his country. Qaddafi believed his nation was being exploited by the west. The oil companies doing business with Libya became a prime target of his anger.

Unlike most other Arab oil states, Libya did business with more than one oil company. Qaddafi decided to play them off against each other. He started with the smallest, Occidental Petroleum. Qaddafi informed Armand Hammer, the president of Occidental, that his oil allocation had been cut by 300,000 barrels a day. Hammer immediately offered a modest price increase for the oil to get the decision reversed. Qaddafi considered the price increase too small and the order for the cutback was not altered.

FIGURE 3

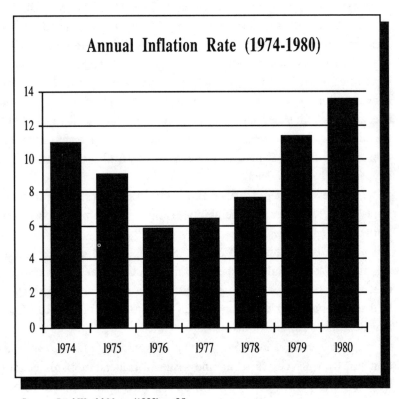

Source: *Real World Macro*(1990), p. 95.

Hammer figured he had an ace in the hole and he now tried to play it. Though Occidental wasn't one of the seven sisters, Hammer thought one of the big oil companies would help him out. After all, it was in their interest to prevent any Arab state from dictating prices. If Qaddafi succeeded, others Arab oil producers might follow suit. Hammer turned to Exxon for help. Unfortunately, he was not one of Exxon's favorite people. Years earlier when Peru had nationalized Exxon's oil fields, Hammer had approached Peru with an offer to have his company step in and run the fields for the government. Exxon had not forgotten his attempt to line his pockets at its expense. Hammer was told he'd get no oil from Exxon to make up for the Libyan cutback. He was on his own.

Hammer was forced to meet Qaddafi's demand for 30 cents more per barrel. Having cowed Occidental, Qaddafi turned his attention to the other oil companies in Libya, picking them off, one by one. By 1971, Libyan oil was selling for $3 a barrel, up 76 cents from a year earlier.

Qaddafi's success spread confidence throughout OPEC. The organization's spokesman, the Saudi Sheik Yamani, urged OPEC members to play hardball with the oil companies. Many did, gaining modest price increase concessions. Then, in 1973, on the Jewish holiday of Yom Kipper, Egyptian forces invaded Israel from the west while Syrian soldiers marched in from the north. Both Arab states received military support from Jordan and Libya during the assault. Israel beat back the invaders, but only after heavy losses.

The U.S., perceived as Israel's allay, again became a target of Arab frustration. It unified the Arab members of OPEC. Sheik Yamani demanded a doubling of the price of oil. When the big oil companies refused, OPEC mounted a boycott aimed primarily at the Americans. The boycott was successful. Oil imports dropped to nearly zero in the U.S. Shortages caused long lines at gas stations. The oil companies were forced to bargain with OPEC and the price of oil quadrupled in the four months before the boycott was finally called off. OPEC now dictated the price of its oil.[22]

The price of oil continued to climb throughout the rest of the decade, with another sharp increase in 1979 that pushed the price to $32 per barrel. From 1974 to 1980, OPEC countries accumulated excess revenues of over $300 billion. In Saudi Arabia alone, oil revenues increased by 2,500 percent.[23] And America was responsible for a good deal of that amount. In the U.S., the bill for imported oil rose from $48 billion in 1972 to $80 billion in 1980. The consequence of this dramatic increase in energy costs meant added inflation.

WAGES

Inflation between 1974 and 1980 average 9.2 percent, and never dropped below 5.8 percent. The trouble with persistent inflation is that people begin to adjust to rather than fight it. Workers in strong unions demanded cost of living allowances (COLAs) in addition to wage increases to stay ahead of inflation. While most other workers found their real income (income adjusted for inflation) constantly eroding, workers in strong unions saw their real incomes increase sharply. From 1967 to 1978, the real income of steelworkers increased by 34.9 percent. Coal miners enjoyed a 31.1 percent rise in income, auto workers a 25.4 percent increase, and the real income of truck drivers increased by 22.9 percent. These far above average wages in steel, coal, autos and transportation were passed on to the consumer, fueling inflation further.

RISING UNEMPLOYMENT

The Ford administration (1974-76) did little to halt inflation. And for most of the Carter administration (1976-80), economic policy aggravated it. Despite the high prices, Carter was more concerned with rising unemployment than with inflation. He had good reason to worry. The baby boomers were joining the workforce in huge numbers. Only a booming economy could have accommodated all of them. But economic growth averaged only 2.3 percent between 1975 and 1980. Hardly enough to qualify as a boom. And certainly not enough to prevent unemployment which was over eight percent in 1975 and remained at about seven percent until 1978.

To combat unemployment Carter used deficit spending to stimulate the economy, and encouraged the Fed to increase the money supply—both inflationary policies. Economic growth quickened slightly, but so did inflation. Finally, by 1979 Carter realized something had to be done about inflation. He asked the Fed to reduce the money supply and got Congress to agree to a reduction in spending. The economy contracted slightly but inflation continued to climb.

By a margin of 9.7 percent of the popular vote, Reagan defeated Carter in the 1980 presidential race on the promise he would end inflation, cut federal spending, and reduce taxes. While inflation worried a lot of people, Reagan's pledge to reduce taxes proved extremely attractive to most Americans.

INFLATION AND TAXES

Actually, inflation and high taxes were closely linked. The progressivity of the income tax dictated that the higher one's income, the larger the percentage of it subject to taxation. The effect of this under rising inflation was to place millions of individuals in a higher tax bracket whenever their wages were increased to keep pace with rising prices. Indeed, keeping up with inflation meant only that real wages, that is wages adjusted for inflation, didn't decline.

Yet while many workers did keep up, because of bracket creep (higher income forcing tax payers into higher tax brackets), more of their pay was deducted for taxes. This resulted in stagnant or declining real incomes for millions of Americans (see Figure 4). In fact, in 1979, the average weekly takehome pay in constant dollars for a worker with three dependents was lower than it was in 1965, $89.49 compared to $91.67.

To make matters worse, higher prices meant whatever takehome pay was left purchased less. In particular, necessities like food and housing consumed a larger share of the family budget than a decade earlier. Like most necessities, food prices soared during the 1970s. And the cost of housing soared. Between 1970 and 1976 the median price of a new home rose by 89 percent.

Many workers found it difficult if not impossible to maintain a middle class standard of living with only one wage earner in the family. It is no accident that women began to enter the workforce in record numbers during the 1970s. Perhaps some were responding to the siren call of women's liberation, but for many the decision to work full time while raising a family was a matter of grim economic necessity. Without an extra paycheck, the family would be forced to accept a lower standard of living. Ironically, recourse to two paychecks to make up for income lost to taxes invariably pushed families into even higher tax brackets. It seemed there was no way to beat the system.

FIGURE 4

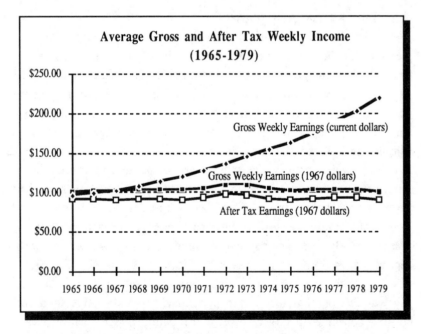

Source: Paul Blumberg, *Inequality in an Age of Decline* (New York: Oxford University Press, 1980), p. 68.

It should therefore come as no surprise that, when Reagan promised to lower taxes and end inflation, his popularity soared.

While the nation waited to see if Reagan would follow through on his campaign promises, the Fed, with President Reagan's approval,[24] decided to fight inflation on its own by continuing to restrict the growth of money. Between 1981 and 1982, the Fed cut the growth of money from 9.9 to 8.8 percent. With money scarce, banks inevitably increased its price. Interest rates ballooned. In late 1981, short term business loans were over 20 percent. In reaction, businesses borrowed less. So did consumers. Sales lagged. As the economy spiralled down into a recession many firms couldn't afford short term loans to see them through. Bankruptcies mounted. Workers in large and small firms were laid off.

THE FED MAKES ITS MOVE

BREAKING THE UNIONS

But what Paul Volker, Chairman of the Fed, wanted most was big layoffs in industries where unions were the strongest—in steel, autos, and mining. While common sense might have suggested that record high oil prices, government policies like deficit spending and the Fed's own decision in the late 1960s to monetize the debt and in the 1970s to accelerate the growth of money, were largely responsible for incessant inflation, Volker was nevertheless convinced the principal cause of inflation was high wages in industries where unions were particularly powerful. And he was willing to put the squeeze on money until it broke these unions.[25] With massive layoffs, union labor would be forced to accept reduced wages if they wanted to go back to work.

PAIN

There were six million unemployed in 1979. By the end of 1982 that number stood at twelve million—nearly 10 percent of all workers. Volker got his wish. The big unions were in disarray. He had broken the power of labor by causing the worst recession since the Great Depression of the 1930s. The Fed caused a great deal of pain, but it got what it wanted—a major reduction in inflation. From a high of 13.5 percent in 1980 it plummeted to 6.1 percent in 1982.

The recession might have lasted even longer if the Fed had its way. However, in 1983, Mexico appealed to the U.S. government to help out with its debt problem. The sharp rise in oil prices during the 1970s had led Mexico to borrow billions to develop its own oil fields. Much of the money came from American banks. Unfortunately, by 1983 the price of oil had declined and Mexican oil wasn't earning enough revenue to meet the interest payments on huge loans from U.S. banks. The U.S. provided the necessary funds to Mexico so it could make the interest payments on its loans. This had the unintended consequence of increasing the money supply. Mexico's loan payments wound up in U.S. banks, increasing the amount of money available for loans and, in time, enlarging the money supply. The growth in the money supply shot up from 8.8 to 11.8 percent. For a brief period, tight money was no longer the rule. Nominal interest rates declined and investment in the economy picked up. The recovery was on its way.

However, in 1984, the Fed stepped on the monetary breaks again and kept them on throughout the rest of the decade to prevent a resurgence of inflation. By then, taxes had been cut and government spending increased, providing a hefty stimulus in demand to keep the recovery going despite the Fed's tight money policy aimed at controlling inflation. And inflation was held low during and after the recovery. It actually dropped down to 1.9 percent in 1986 and has not gone above 4.8 since. Perhaps 4.8 percent is still too high compared with the extremely low inflation rates of the 1950s and 1960s, but the inflation shock of the 1970s has forced many to lower their expectations. Today, anything under five percent is greeted as price stabilization.

HELPING OUT THE BANKS

One other action of the Fed deserves mention. It decided to keep interest rates high. While tight money naturally pushes interest rates up, if the Fed wants it is able to keep them artificially high by manipulating the Federal Funds rate.

Often banks find themselves right at the edge of their reserve requirement. They can either cease making more loans, or get more money so they have more reserves. The latter requires borrowing from other banks with excess reserves or directly from the Fed. The Fed can influence the rate of interest charged for extra reserves by raising or lowering its own rate to borrowers, or by reducing or raising the level of reserves of the large banks who do most of the short term reserve lending in what is known as the Federal Funds market. If the Fed keeps those reserves low, large banks naturally charge more to other banks for borrowing from these scarce funds.

The Federal Funds rate is the prevailing interest rate for additional reserve money, and is watched closely by financial institutions as a guide for setting short term interest rates. When the Fed keeps it high, it translates into high interest rates for loans, such as the prime rate—the interest rate charged by commercial banks to corporate customers.[26]

Not only did the Fed keep interest rates high during the 1981-1983 recession, making things difficult for a recovery because borrowed money for investment was so expensive (though the recovery was very robust despite this impediment), it also kept them high after the recovery and throughout the rest of the decade.

On the face of it, this was an odd thing to do, especially once inflation declined. With sharp inflation, high interest rates make sense. At a 12 percent interest on loans and a 11 percent inflation rate, the real interest earned by banks is only 1 percent when adjusted for inflation. Banks certainly have a right to be concerned about earning a decent real interest rate. But what is decent? The average real interest rate for the three decades between 1950 and 1979 was only 1.7 percent. It was just

1.3 percent in the 1950s, climbed to 3 percent in the 1960s and dropped to 1 percent in the 1970s. Even if the halcyon banking days of the 1960s were used as a benchmark, banks should expect no more than a 3 percent real interest rate as fair.

FIGURE 5

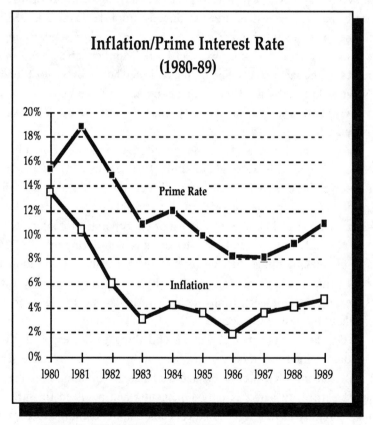

Source: *Real World Macro*, 7th ed., p. 95

However, when tight money reduced inflation in 1981 from 13.5 percent to 10.4 percent, the Fed didn't adjust the interest rate to 13.4 percent to provide banks 3 percent real interest. Instead it pushed it up to 18.9 percent creating a real interest rate of 8.5 percent. In 1982, the real interest rate went even higher, to 8.8 percent. In fact, for the rest of the decade the annual real interest rate never fell below 5.2 percent, and averaged about 6.8 percent between 1981-1989 (Figure 5).

What was behind the Fed's manipulation of interest rates? One thing behind it was the desire to allow banks to play catch up for the bad decade of the 1970s. They had suffered for a decade with a dismal 1 percent real interest rate. They would need high real interest to make up the loss. Apparently the Fed decided a rate twice as high as enjoyed in the 1960s would just about do it. But the policy also favored anyone earning income in financial markets. Indeed, after just four years of the Fed's high interest policy, personal income earned from interest grew by more than 70 percent.[27] People with money were being made even richer. The extent of this phenomenon is now only just being appreciated, and we will take a closer look at it later on.

Another reason the Fed decided to keep interest rates high was the realization that the Reagan administration was willing to run very large deficits. The worry was that big deficits could cause problems with inflation. More particularly, there was little desire at the Fed to repeat the mistake made during the Johnson administration. Then the Fed provided the president a cheap solution to the deficit problem by monetizing the debt. But writing checks to cover the Reagan deficits would expand the money supply and stimulate inflation—just the opposite of what the Fed wanted to do. Reducing inflation was at the top of its agenda. So the Fed decided the deficit would have to be financed by borrowing from private financial markets. However, to allay the administration's fears that government borrowing to cover the deficit might crowd out borrowing for normal business investment and limit economic growth, the Fed committed itself to a policy of high interest rates. It was believed this would essentially circumvent the crowding problem,[28] because high interest rates would attract foreign capital, guaranteeing plenty of money seeking high interest government bonds with more than enough left over from both foreign and domestic sources to finance normal investment needs.

This decision would later have momentous consequences for the federal budget. As the Fed predicted, high interest rates did guarantee that there was always plenty of foreign capital to cover government borrowing, but the high rates also dramatically increased government's cost for this borrowing. From one year to the next, the amount of the annual interest payment on the debt grew to record proportions until it eventually became one of the largest items of the federal budget, eventually equaling the entire annual deficit itself. To some it seemed like something out of *Alice in Wonderland*. One reason the deficit was so large was because the bill for financing earlier deficits—the interest payment on the national debt—had become so high. Indeed, the more government borrowed, the more funds it had to earmark for paying the interest on the national debt, and the less borrowed money was able to be spent on other things. Eventually, nearly every cent the government borrowed went to pay for the interest on the national debt. It had to run a deficit to pay for the deficit. The faster the government ran, the more it stood still.

NOTES

[1]The Committee for Economic Development played an important role in this development. Formed by the Department of Commerce in 1942, its members were prominent business leaders who accepted the fact that public opinion supported government involvement in the economy, but believed this demand could be satisfied without granting politicians extraordinary power to alter the course of the economy. They envisaged the concept of stabilizers as they key to de-politicizing fiscal and monetary policy.

[2]Lawrence Brewster, *The Public Agenda: Issues in American Politics* (New York: St. Martin's Press, 1987), p. 22.

[3]James Fallows, *National Defense* (New York: Vintage Books, 1981), p. 4.

[4]Lawrence Brewster, *The Public Agenda* , p. 261.

[5]The words are Paul Warnke's, quoted in Hedrick Smith, *The Power Game* (New York: Ballantine Books, 1988), p. 181.

[6]Seymour Melman, *The Permanent War Economy* (New York: Touchstone Book, 1985), p. 134.

[7]Adam Yarmolinsky, *The Military Establishment* (New York: Harper Colophon Books, 1971), p.61.

[8]Economists have estimated that 45 percent of U.S. economic growth between 1929 and 1969 was the result of technological innovation alone. See Paul Blumberg, *Inequality in an Age of Decline* (Oxford: Oxford University Press, 1981), p. 144.

[9]Melman, *The Permanent War Economy*, p. 92.

[10]Ibid., p. 93.

[11]Weintraub, *Our Stagflation Malaise* , p. 148.

[12]Derived from data in *Statistical Abstract of the United States* (1990), p. 585.

[13]Harry Summers, *Vietnam War Almanac* (New York: Facts On File Publications, 1985), p. 91.

[14]Ibid., p. 100.

[15]Statistical Abstract of the United States (1990), p. 336. Some estimates place the figure much higher, at about $600 billion, after factoring in the cost of veteran benefits and interest paid on the war debt. See Richard Severo and Lewis Milford, The Wages of War (New York: Simon and Schuster, 1989), p. 348.

[16]Ezra Solomon, *Beyond the Turning Point* (San Francisco: W.H. Freeman and Company, 1982), p. 62.

[17]*Real World Macro*, 5th ed. (Somerville, MA: Economic Affairs Bureau, Inc., 1990), p. 95.

[18]Herbert Stein, *Presidential Economics*, 2nd ed. (Washington, D.C.: American Enterprise Institute, 1988), p. 156.

[19]Solomon, *Beyond the Turning Point* , p. 73.

[20]Frank Levy, *Dollars and Dreams* (New York: W. W. Norton and Company, 1988), p. 61.

[21]Dankwart Rustow, *Oil and Turmoil* (New York: W.W. Norton and Company, 1982), p. 53.

[22]David Halberstam, *The Reckoning*, pp. 451-459.; John Blair, *The Control of Oil* (New York: Vintage Books, 1978), pp. 211-234.

[23]Ragaei El Mallakh, *Saudi Arabia: Rush to Development—Profile of an Energy Economy and Investment* (Baltimore: The Johns Hopkins University Press, 1982), p. 61.

[24]Greider, *Secrets of the Temple* , p. 542.

[25]Ibid., p. 429.

[26]Ibid., pp. 62-63.

[27]Ibid., p. 578.

[28]Ibid., p. 561.

Chapter 8
Reagan

While the Fed managed the money supply in pursuit of its own ends—and with Reagan's approval—the President undertook to enact a fiscal revolution to revitalize the economy.

THE ATTACK ON BIG GOVERNMENT

During his presidential campaign, Reagan blamed government for nearly all of the problems of the economy. He claimed government had grown too large and become too costly. It had interfered too much with the economy, strangling business innovation with senseless and expensive regulations. He also claimed taxes on both businesses and wage earners had become exorbitant. According to Reagan, high taxes were eroding business profits and destroying the incentive to reinvest in the economy. And because of high personal income taxes, the takehome pay of workers was shrinking yearly. The solution to all these problems, he argued, was simple: reduce taxes and shrink government.

It was a scathing condemnation of the federal government. However, it bore little relation to fact. Consider the charge that government had grown too large. In terms of federal outlays as a percent of GNP, government had grown only slightly in the previous twenty years, and had actually begun to decline in size from 1975 to 1979 (see Figure 6). In 1970, federal outlays were 20.3 percent of GNP. In 1979, they were only slightly higher at 20.7 percent. To be sure, federal outlays had grown appreciably in the two decades before Reagan's election, but so had the GNP. On the whole, federal outlays simply kept pace with GNP growth. Understood in this way, federal expenditures had remained relatively steady. They did not expand out of control as Reagan charged.

Nor had the federal government become bloated with employees. In absolute numbers there had been some growth to be sure. In 1970, total civilian federal employees amounted to 2.89 million. By 1979 that number had increased modestly to 2.91 million. However, when measured as a percentage of the total workforce, the size of the federal bureaucracy had actually declined, from 3.7 percent of all employed workers in 1970 to 2.9 percent in 1979.[1] In short, the increase in federal employees did not keep pace with the general growth in non-government employment.

FIGURE 6

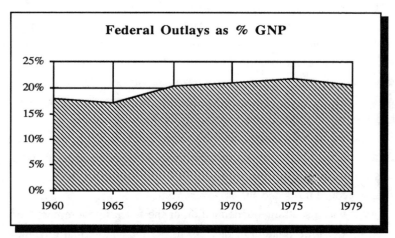

Sources: *U.S. Statistical Abstract* (1990), p. 312, *Real World Macro*, 7th ed., p. 91, *The Budget of the United States Government (1981)*, p. 614

And what about taxes? Reagan claimed they were too high. In fact, business taxes had been declining for two decades, not increasing. At the start of the 1960s, corporations paid about 45 percent of profits in taxes. In 1970, this declined to 42.4 percent. It dropped again to 27.3 percent in 1975, and declined even further to 25.9 percent in 1980.[2]

Unlike corporate taxes, personal income taxes did not decline between 1960 and 1979. However, they did not increase as dramatically as Reagan suggested. In fact, for middle and low income families (the majority of Americans) the percentage of family income going to federal income tax increased only slightly during this period. For example, in 1960, a middle income family paid 13.7 percent of family income in income taxes. In 1979 the figure was still only 14 percent.[3]

The reason middle and lower income families fared so well even in the 1970s when inflation was steadily increasing was that they were protected from bracket creep by several tax reductions favoring families at or below the median income.[4]

On the other hand, families with incomes above that level did not do so well. They paid a higher percentage of their income in taxes. Coupled with inflation, these higher taxes had made it more difficult for such families to maintain a middle-class standard of living. This certainly proved daunting to families with two income earners trying to edge into the upper middle-class. Higher taxes made this very difficult. Indeed, for many it seemed two incomes were needed to prevent a decline in their family's standard of living. Nevertheless, for a large percentage of Americans taxes were not a growing burden.

Not only was the size of government (measured in either expenditures or personnel) nor the tax rate as disturbing as Reagan claimed, the economy had actually performed much better than he was willing to admit. Between 1950 and 1960 the GNP increased by 38.35 percent. In the next decade, a time when dreaded Keynesian economics dominated policy making, the GNP grew again by an impressive 45.09 percent. Even in the so-called bad 1970s, the GNP continued to grow, increasing by 31.91 percent over the decade. The economy had performed well enough to convince people to invest in its future. Private investment in the economy averaged 15.4 percent of GNP in the 1960s and 14.8 percent in the 1970s. In 1979 it actually jumped to 16.3 percent.[5] This was less than the 17 percent average of the 1950s, but very respectable given historical trends.

And what about excessive regulation of the economy? Reagan's prime target here was pollution control arising out of earlier clean air and water acts and legislation dealing with the disposal of toxic waste. These environmental regulations were costly, but during the 1970s Japan was spending more as a percent of its GNP than the U.S. to clean up its environment. And West Germany was devoting about the same percent of its GNP as the U.S.[6] Both nations were economic successes. And apparently neither felt the extra cost of anti-pollution regulations were too high to justify the expense.

The economy of the 1970s did have problems: unemployment and inflation. But it is doubtful government policy was mainly responsible for either of them. For example, high unemployment was not the consequence of poor economic performance. It was the result of the baby-boom generation entering the job market—more than two million per year. Between 1965 and 1980, nearly 30 million new workers joined the economy. This was equal to about half the entire labor force of Japan. Never had the U.S. economy been forced to absorb so many workers, both in absolute numbers or as a percent of the total workforce. Only unprecedented growth would have created enough jobs for all of the new workers. There was growth, but it was hardly unprecedented. So there was unemployment. But demographics, not failed economic policy, was the root cause. In fact, the economic growth of the Reagan years was even less than in the 1970s. Had Reagan's policies dominated that earlier decade, unemployment would have been even higher.

On the other hand, government policy was to blame for some of the inflation that occurred during the 1970s. Certainly President Johnson's decision to monitize the Vietnam War deficits gave inflation its start, but other factors also contributed to the rising inflation, most beyond the control of government. There was the sharp rise in oil prices, crop failures, and inflation abroad. Remove these factors and the inflation rate would not have been so high. What is more important, government's ability to deal effectively with inflation was severely constrained by the large numbers of baby boomers entering the workforce. Reducing spending, or raising taxes, or restricting the money supply would all have reduced jobs and increased the already high level of unemployment. The administrations of Nixon, Ford, and Carter decided that, under the unique circumstances, providing jobs was a higher priority than reducing inflation.

Reagan, on the other hand, talked as if the baby boom never existed, and that past policies which tried to grapple with unprecedent demographics were completely irresponsible. Nor did he acknowledge other important facts. Government had not grown to outrageous proportions. Taxes had not increased out of sight. Economic growth had not lagged, nor had investment in the economy dried up. Nevertheless, he presumed all of this had occurred. And he turned to a new economics that shared this false presumption, required it to make sense. Unfortunately, since Reagan's new economics was based on false premises, it was bound to fail. It assumed taxes were too high, government was too big, and investment was drying up, and devised strategies for turning things around. The new economics was called "supply-side economics".

SUPPLY-SIDE MAGIC

Reagan wanted to reduce taxes and dramatically increase defense spending. Normally, the consequences of such a policy would be large deficits which would exacerbate inflation. But Reagan believed a large tax cut would act as powerful stimulus for investment in the economy. And he was convinced, less on factual evidence and more as a matter of faith in the wealth creating genius of entrepreneurs, their pockets crammed full with newly acquired venture capital freed up by lower taxes, that the ensuing economic growth would be so great that it would both reduce inflation and increase tax revenues.

Growth would reduce inflation because with so many more goods produced at the same quantity of money, the price for goods would have to fall. With only so much money available for spending, and a larger quantity of goods to purchase, sellers would have to drop prices if they wanted to clear their shelves of inventory.

And tax revenues would increase because with so much more growth there would be more people employed. More taxpayers translates into additional tax revenue. Also, because of economic growth, workers would earn more on average, increasing their total tax bill. So even at a lower tax rate, the total tax revenue taken in would be greater than when taxes were higher. In fact, the Kennedy tax cuts had achieved pretty much the same thing, though the Reaganites weren't too eager to draw support from the successes of a Democratic President for their plan. Anyway, Kennedy was a Keynesian. Reagan rejected Keynesianism, which meant he had to call his program by a different name.

Reagan offered the American public a rosy picture. The label for it was supply side economics. The Keynesians had always emphasized the demand side of the economy, concentrating on it to the detriment of nearly everything else. The supply-siders, inspired by the writings of U.S.C. economist Arthur Laffer and his journalist disciple, Jude Wanniski, turned the spotlight from the consumer and directed it on the producer of the goods and services—the supplier. The real source of economic growth, they argued, was here. And all it took to get the engine of growth revving was to provide producers an incentive to produce—a chance to make decent profits. But high taxes destroy that incentive. They eat away at profits. Eventually, profits decline so far businessmen lack all incentive to invest in growth. Some may even retire from the competition.

This was not a new idea. Back in 1756, the philosopher David Hume, who in addition to writing treatises on morality and epistemology liked to dabble in what was then called political economy, observed that:

> Exorbitant taxes, like extreme necessity, destroy industry by producing despair; and even before they reach this pitch, they raise the wages of the labourer and manufacturer, and heighten the price of all commodities. An attentive disinterested legislature will observe the point when the emolument ceases and the prejudice begins.7

Of course, businessmen didn't need a philosopher or an economist to tell them high taxes are a bad idea. They had been complaining about them for years.

In theory, at least, the idea had some merit. Obviously if government taxed away nearly all the profits of businesses, most would eventually close their doors. Even short of that point many businesses might delay investment in new plants or equipment because of perceived low after tax profit margins. So the theory did make some sense. The problem was no one offered evidence for determining when taxes had become too high. In fact, though taxes on wage earners had certainly increased (along with their earnings), taxes on businesses had actually declined over the years. Wasn't this incentive enough to keep businessmen busy expanding the economy?

Not according to the supply-siders. Businessmen also need plenty of venture capital to fuel investment. And this was being taxed away. It was people with high incomes, those who supposedly groaned under the burden of a progressive tax system, who normally save the most and provide the money for investment. But taxes siphoned away the money that would have gone into savings. The solution was not only to lower taxes on corporate profits but to also lower them on personal income. With this accomplished, high income Americans would suddenly have more extra cash to save and invest. The economy would be awash in venture capital, and farsighted entrepreneurs would sop it up. Old businesses would expand, new ones would be created. The GNP would explode.

So just lower taxes and all of our economic woes would go away. There would be little unemployment because a growing economy would need every available worker to keep it going. And inflation would disappear because the volume of goods would outstrip the volume of money.

One difficulty with this idea was that in the existing economy its predictions were unrealistic. Take inflation. When Reagan assumed office, demand for goods and services was growing at about 12 percent per year. To increase economic growth to match or exceed this figure, in essence to out-produce demand and eliminate inflation, would require both a dramatic increase in total output plus an equally robust increase in worker productivity.[8] Economic growth in the range of 8 percent per year and a doubling of worker productivity might do the trick, but such figures were wildly unrealistic. In fact, increases in economic growth and worker productivity throughout the 1980s never even came close.

Of course, inflation did decline, but it had nothing to do with Reagan's fiscal policy, or supply side effects of tax reduction. The Fed simply acted independently, keeping the growth of the money supply low, and interest rates high, to dampen inflation. Indeed, Reagan's economic policy was essentially Keynesian, though in a strange form. Fiscal and monetary policy worked at cross purposes. Tax cuts and increased spending stimulated demand, and tight money reduced it. The result was modest growth with modest inflation—and huge budget deficits.

DEFICIT SPENDING

Since massive growth predictions never materialized, tax revenues didn't increase enough to come even close to wiping out the budget deficit. Over the years, only tax payers earning more than $200,000 wound up paying more total income taxes than prior to the tax cut, and only because their incomes had shot out of sight. Total income tax revenues from everyone else declined.[9] Inevitably, the deficit continued to grow.

NOT A HEAD FOR FIGURES

David Stockman, Reagan's appointee to head the Office of Management and Budget, and a dedicated supply-sider, was assigned the task of implementing the Reagan revolution. At first he was optimistic. Then he looked at the numbers. They didn't add up. You couldn't have massive increases in military spending (adding up to a total $1.5 trillion in seven years) and reduced taxes without causing huge deficits.

Nevertheless, Reagan remained convinced that tax cuts would generate the economic growth to solve the problem. But Stockman insisted that even if the growth materialized sometime down the line, in the near future there would be large deficits unless huge cuts were made in the budget.

The problem was that neither the President nor Congress was willing to make the cuts. The big ticket items in domestic spending were Social Security, veterans benefits, and Medicare. No one wanted to cut those because of fear of voter backlash. A lot of people received those benefits, and most of them voted. Stockman concluded that the Republicans as well as the Democrats in Congress and even Reagan's own team liked the welfare state and had no intention of dismantling it if it might cost them votes. In fact, after months of wrangling, Stockman could get only minor reductions in the budget.

Stockman continued to warn the President of the impending massive deficits, but Reagan couldn't comprehend the numbers. Stockman finally realized the President really didn't understand economics. He thought in anecdotes—incidents that had occurred in his own life, or simple stories about friends and family, that illustrated some general point. It didn't matter that they were often irrelevant to the matter at hand. It was simply the way the President's mind worked. Complicated facts and figures were beyond him, and abstract theory made his eyes glaze over. What did catch his attention, though, was simple-minded presentations employing cartoon characters.

For some time Stockman had been doing battle with the Secretary of Defense, Casper Weinberger, to get him to slow down the growth in defense expenditures. At one meeting, Weinberger was able to destroy Stockman's sophisticated charts and graphs with a simple presentation that won the President over to his side.

> Weinberger had ... brought with him a blown-up cartoon. It showed three soldiers. One was a pigmy who carried no rifle. He represented the Carter budget. The second was a four-eyed wimp who looked like Woody Allen, carrying a tiny rifle. That was—me?—the OMB defense budget. Finally there was G.I. Joe himself, 190 pounds of fighting man, all decked out in helmet and flak jacket and pointing an M-60 machine gun menacingly at—me again? This imposing warrior represented, yes, the Department of Defense budget plan.[10]

Stockman couldn't believe what he was seeing. Of Weinberger he says: "Did he think the White House was on Sesame Street?"[11] As it turned out, that was precisely what Weinberger believed, and to Stockman's chagrin, he was right.

THE BITTER FRUIT OF POLITICAL REFORM

Stockman's frustration is understandable. But, he should have known better. For some time, American politics had been undergoing a profound transformation. Congress in particular had pretty much lost the capacity to deal with the public interest broadly conceived. Instead it had become a fragmented body concerned primarily with satisfying the demands of local constituents and powerful private interests.

Enabling Acts

Stockman was aware of this change. In his book, *The Triumph of Politics*, he acknowledges the scholarly work by political scientists like Theodore Lowi documenting the transfer of political power from Congress to private interests.[12] According to Lowi, rather than deciding policy on its own as the Constitution stipulates, Congress has progressively abandoned this role and instead transferred it to the federal bureaucracy and the special interests it serves. Over the decades, legislation has become more abstract. Instead of directing bureaus and agencies to undertake specific concrete tasks guided by precise and clear rules, Congress passes enabling Acts which state some broad purpose to be achieved and then leaves it to the federal bureaucracy to give the legislation concrete form, and to establish the rules and procedures for its implementation. In sum, Congress merely announces broad goals to be achieved by government and then leaves it to the bureaucracy to fashion the actual policy to achieve those goals.

A good example of this sort of thing is the Economic and Stabilization Act of 1970. This was the piece of legislation authorizing wage and price controls under Nixon. However, the legislation left it to the President to define the actual policy. Here is part of the text of the law (Sections 202 and 203): "The President is authorized to issue such orders and regulations as he may deem appropriate to stabilize prices, rents, wages and salaries. ... The president may delegate the performance of any function under this title to such officers, departments, and agencies of the United States as he may deem appropriate."[13]

The Act gave Nixon the power to stabilize prices, rents, wages and salaries as he saw fit. It was totally up to him. Congress provided absolutely no guidelines, no rules, nothing. The results were predictable. Nixon managed the wage price controls in a selective manner, forcing small business and non-unionized workers to adhere to strict limits, while granting wage raise concessions to big labor and price increases to big business.[14] Groups with power were able to bend the law to their will, those who were powerless were forced to bear the largest sacrifices.

Interest Group Pluralism

With the proliferation of "enabling" type legislation, real political power devolved to federal agencies charged with formulating policies and implementing them. Powerful interest groups quickly moved in to lobby agencies for favors, persuading them to shape policy so it served their interests. Instead of government regulating powerful interests in the national interest, these interests began to dictate policy, using the power of government, the force of law, to advance their particular ends or to protect them from the public. The label for this sort of government is "Interest Group Pluralism." It has been going on for so long it is now viewed by many as the natural way to conduct politics.

Even groups opposed to government by private interests have felt obliged to adapt to the rules of the game to defend what they conceive as the public interest. The environmental movement foundered until it organized into interest groups focusing on various environmental issues. For those concerned with preserving and expanding wilderness areas and maintaining our national parks, there is the Sierra Club and Wilderness Society. If you think conversion to solar power will help protect the environment from pollution you can turn to the Solar Lobby. People interested in protecting wild animals have the Fund for Animals and the

Society for Animal Protective Legislation to advance the cause. The number of organized environmental groups are legion: Natural Resources Defense Council, National Audubon Society, National Wildlife Federation, Izaak Walton League, Friends of the Earth, Environmental Policy Center, Environmental Defense Fund, Environmental Action, etc. Each organization raises money for its cause, hires lobbyists, contributes money to campaigns, and presses its case before the appropriate Congressional committee or federal agency with policy making authority over some particular area of the environment. In short, they behave just like other powerful interest groups, each pressing its claim because it is organized and powerful, not because it has some special insight into the public interest.

For example, in the early 1980s when under pressure from automobile manufacturers the Senate Environment and Public Works Committee considered amending the Clean Air Act to relax standards on carbon monoxide emissions from autos, the committee was besieged by experienced lobbyists from the National Clean Air Coalition who succeeded in having the proposal tabled.[15] Had the Coalition not been as well organized as the auto industry, and experienced with the rules of the game, it would not have had a chance of success.

Political Reform

The tendency of interest group pluralism to bend politics to the service of narrow private interests rather than the public interest was increased by three political reforms. In the early 1970s, the Democratic party decided to reform delegate selection for the national party convention whose main task is to select the party's candidate for President. The complaint was that state party bosses were controlling delegate selection and denying racial, and ideological, minorities significant representation at the party's national convention. The thrust of the reform was to turn to primaries rather than state conventions or party caucuses for the delegate selection process. This would allow voters to decide which slate of delegates (pledged to a particular candidate) would be sent to the national convention. Prior to the reform, only seventeen states had presidential primaries. After the reform, in 1972, twenty-three states had primaries. Because Democrats were often forced to change state law to establish a presidential primary election, Republicans in these states were usually forced into primaries as well. Today, all but fourteen states hold presidential primaries.

Another important reform was the Federal Election Campaign Act Amendments of 1974. This was in response to the campaign finance scandal of Nixon's second presidential campaign. The existence of millions in illegal campaign funds was uncovered during the Watergate investigations concerning President Nixon's efforts to cover up White House duplicity in the attempted burglary of the Democratic national party headquarters in the Watergate building complex in Washington, D.C., as well as the use of the FBI and CIA to harass Nixon's "political enemies". In an attempt to diminish the importance of campaign contributions in presidential elections, the Campaign Act established federal campaign funding for Presidential candidates.

The combination of an increase in the number of states conducting presidential primaries and the federal subsidy for Presidential candidates greatly reduced, if not eliminated, the influence of state and national party leaders in the selection of Presidential candidates. In the main, politicians running for President have relied on their own personal campaign organizations and the money from federal subsidies and ignored party leaders. Once elected, the President owes very little to his party, and his links to party leaders are much more tenuous than in the past. The problem with this is that every President needs the support of his party in Congress to pass legislation. Reestablishing lost links takes time and can damage the possibility of success of major legislative packages. This was certainly the experience of the Carter Presidency,[16] less true of the Reagan years. On the other hand, today even if a President has good relations with party leaders in Congress, it is doubtful this can guarantee support for major changes in legislation, especially if such changes require drastic cuts in the budget.

Decline of Party Discipline

Party discipline in Congress has pretty much disappeared. Like Presidential candidates, individual Congressmen now owe very little to their party. Also like Presidential candidates, they have their own campaign organizations, and raise their own campaign money. Part of this change is due to another provision of the Federal Election Campaign Act Amendments of 1974. It authorized the creation of Political Action Committees (PACs), permitting corporations, labor unions, and other special interest groups to collect funds for contributions to political candidates. In 1974 there were only 89 corporate PACs, by 1984 there were 1,682. In 1986, political candidates received $132.2 million from PACs. PAC money has become an important source of financing for incumbent Congressmen, making them financially independent from their party. Not needing the party to get reelected, they often vote on bills as they wish rather than as party leaders request.

Subcommittee Dominance

Congress has changed in another way. In the early 1970s, first in the House and later in the Senate, younger Congressmen revolted against senior Congressmen, reducing the importance of seniority for committee chairmanship, and dramatically expanding the number of subcommittees so that nearly every Congressman could chair a subcommittee or serve on a subcommittee that dealt with important matters concerning his or her constituents. The result was a major decentralization of power in Congress. Also, for the first time nearly every Congressman was in a position through subcommittee membership to influence legislation that would benefit his constituents.

It was a marvelous system for enhancing each Congressman's reputation with his constituents. If his constituents were farmers he could serve on an important subcommittee deciding agricultural policy and guarantee that the local farmers received some sort of farm subsidy or benefit. If there were defense contractors in his district, he could serve on a defense committee and help insure his district got its share of defense contracts. Congressmen became more constituent oriented than ever before. The old system where Congressmen supported each other's bills to benefit constituents at home because it made reelection easier, was now intensified. Voters responded predictably; they returned incumbents to office, election after election. Today, with a reelection rate of about 97 percent, a member of the House is replaced only after he or she retires or dies in office.

Of course, the size of the budget naturally increased to accommodate all of this "pork". Before the Reagan tax cuts, voters complained loudly about free spending politicians while at the same time voting for another term for their own Congressman whose free spending was perceived as responsible representation.

The difficulty with all of this is that Congressman are now preoccupied with serving local constituents, or powerful interest groups who help fund their campaigns, to the detriment of the national interest. As former House Speaker Tip O'Neill put it not long ago, members today "no longer have to follow the national philosophy of the party. They can get re-elected ... on how they serve their constituents."[17] Consequently, when Reagan asked for major budget cuts, even the members of his own party in the House and Senate refused to go along. Major cuts would mean doing away with some benefit they had worked hard to get for their constituents. Reagan didn't elect them, party leaders had no control over them. They were responsible only to a small group of people—the voters back home. If serving the interests of this relatively small number of people meant sacrificing the national interest, then so be it. Consequently, the appeal of party leaders for Congressmen to direct their attention to national problems, and the general public interest, fell on deaf ears. This should not have surprised Stockman who served in the House himself before joining Reagan's team in the White House.

TAX CUTS
While the Reagan administration did little to trim the budget, and actually increased its size because of the massive defense build-up, it nevertheless moved ahead full speed to get Congress to cut taxes. Twice.

Economic Recovery Tax Act (1981)
The first tax reduction came in 1981 with the Economic Recovery Tax Act. The Act phased in a three year tax cut of 5 percent the first year, and 10 percent per annum for the next two years.

People with high incomes received the largest benefits. The top bracket for taxes was reduced from 70 to 50 percent, a twenty percent gain for the wealthiest income earners in America. The tax rate on capital gains (income from the sale of property, stocks, bonds, etc.) was dropped from 28 to 20 percent. Not only did the Act reduce the personal income tax, it established indexing so that inflation couldn't cause bracket creep. If inflation increased, tax rates would be lowered accordingly to take that into account. Corporate taxes were also reduced and depreciation benefits liberalized. In 1980, corporate income tax receipts represented 12.5 percent of federal revenue. By 1983, this figure was halved to 6.2 percent.

Tax Increases
Despite his endless public chant to never increase taxes, Reagan nevertheless signed into law a modest tax increase for 1984. The deficit was growing so fast he had to do something to quiet anxious critics. Actually, an earlier tax increase had already occurred in 1983. Reagan could get off the hook for this one because it was planned during the Carter administration. The payroll deduction for Social Security was raised from 6.05 to 6.7 percent, an 11 percent increase.[18] Because the tax only applied to the first $35,700 of income, the impact of the tax increase fell more heavily on low income taxpayers. A person earning $25,000

had all of his income taxed at 6.7 percent, but someone earning $70,000 had only half of his income taxed at that amount—reducing his effective Social Security tax rate to 3.35 percent of gross income. Despite the Reagan income tax cut, with the hike in the Social Security tax many low and moderate income households found their total federal taxes higher now than before the income tax reform.

Tax Reform Act of 1986

The second major reduction in taxes occurred with the Tax Reform Act of 1986. Again, people with high incomes benefited most. The top individual tax rate was dropped from 50 to 28 percent. But low income wage earners also benefited. First, the personal exemption (base amount of income immune from tax) was doubled removing approximately 5 million from the tax rolls. Second, a low rate of 15 percent was set for tax payers at the bottom of the income tax ladder.[19]

Growing Deficits

Together, the two tax reductions resulted in $1.15 trillion of lost tax revenue from 1982 to 1990—just about equal to the amount of the deficits for that period.[20]

The size of the deficits became an embarrassment to the Reagan administration. The deficit rose sharply from $127 billion in 1982, to $207.8 billion in 1983 and reached $221.2 billion in 1986. Reagan blamed Congress for failing to limit spending. The Congressional response was the Gramm-Rudman Balanced Budget Act of 1985. Gramm-Rudman sets target figures for deficit limits, scheduled to grow smaller each year until 1991 when the budget is to be balanced. If a target isn't reached, there is to be across the board cuts (excluding Social Security) until the target limit is achieved.

CREATIVE ACCOUNTING

This did not solve the problem. In no year has Congress been able to meet the target figure without engaging in creative accounting. This has relieved Congress and the President of the obligation to reduce spending while deluding the public that the deficit is actually being reduced as stipulated by Gramm-Rudman.

Trust Fund Magic

The creative accounting employed involves counting trust fund surpluses as revenue. Remember the hike in Social Security taxes in 1983. By 1985 this produced a revenue surplus for Social Security. The program was taking in more than it spent. This growing surplus, increasing by about $15 billion per year, has offered a simple way to camouflage the real size of the deficit every year since 1985.

For example, in 1988 the surplus was $38 billion. By using this money for the purchase of Treasury bonds, $38 billion in new revenue suddenly appeared, reducing a $194 billion deficit to $155 billion—much closer to that year's Gramm-Rudman target figure, and leaving Social Security with an I.O.U. from the Treasury that the money will be paid back. And it will have to be paid back because sometime in the early 21st century millions of baby boomers will begin to retire. The surpluses were meant to cover this expected jump in Social Security outlays. Unless the Treasury borrows (more deficits in the future) to pay back the amount it owes the Social Security trust fund, it will have to finance the payback out of new taxes. Sadly, the tax bill will mostly likely fall on the next generation of taxpayers who will be penalized for the creative accounting of the Reagan and Bush years.

FIGURE 7

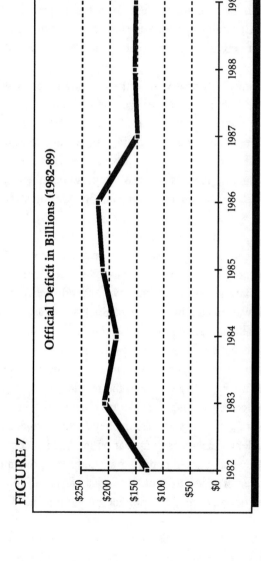

Official Deficit in Billions (1982-89)

Source: *Real World Macro*, 7th ed., p. 95.

Moving Off-Budget

Another way the deficit is disguised is to move items off budget. Off-budget activities are distinguished from those on budget by their revenue source. Generally, the revenue for items on-budget comes from taxes. Off-budget activities are financed from fees or other charges for services.

Debt is handled differently as well. The power to tax is the guarantee that stands behind all on-budget debt. This is what makes government bonds a safe investment. It is a virtual certainty that they will be paid off. If there is not enough incoming tax revenue to cover the cost, taxes can be raised. Off-budget debt is less secure. Since revenue comes from fees and not taxes, there is no absolute guarantee there will always be enough revenue to meet interest payments or retire outstanding bonds at maturity.

In the past, the main reason government units shifted items off budget was to circumvent legislative debt restrictions or voter hostility to new government projects or services. Until recently, going off-budget was a local and state government strategy. Indeed, the first off-budget entity in the U.S. was created by the city of Spokane, Washington in 1895 for the construction and maintenance of a toll bridge.[21]

Most state constitutions set strict limits on the size of government debt. When that limit is reached, it is difficult to undertake new projects requiring debt financing. To get around the restriction, new projects can be moved off-budget by issuing a corporate charter to a new agency or authority to undertake the project. The money for the project, essentially new government debt which doesn't appear on the budget, comes from the agency's sale of revenue-backed bonds. State and local governments have used off-budget enterprises to build libraries, airports and hospitals, supply water and flood control, and provide public transit. The list goes on and on.

State and local governments went off-budget in a big way in the late 1970s when, after a tax rebellion led to the passage of Proposition 13 in

California providing property tax relief, citizen tax revolts spread from state to state throughout the country, many of them placing strict limits on tax rates. Going off-budget was a popular way to get around these limits by replacing government agencies with off-budget entities which collected fees rather than taxes to pay for operations. Citizens still shelled out as much as before for the same services, but since they were paying fees instead of taxes they couldn't complain about high taxes.

Because activities of off-budget enterprises never appear in official government budgets, the growth of such enterprises disguises both the real size of government and its real costs. For example, as of 1977 there were nearly 26,000 off-budget enterprises in the U.S.[22] In 1979, off-budget debt for all state and local governments reached $31.3 billion. Just nine years earlier it had been only $6.1 billion. And in 1983, just one off-budget enterprise in the state of Washington, the Washington Public Power Supply System (WPPSS), had acquired outstanding debt of over $7 billion.

The federal government got into off-budget operations rather late. By 1970 federal off-budget expenditures amounted to no more than $27.6 billion. Until quite recently, most of these off-budget programs were various forms of credit activity, such as the Federal National Mortgage Association (FNMA), Farm Credit Administration (FCA), Federal Home Loan Bank (FHLB), Federal Home Loan Mortgage Corporation (FHLMC) and the Student Loan Marketing Association (SLMA). Then came the huge deficits of the mid-1980s. The expansion of off-budget accounts expanded rapidly as a way to hide the real size of the budget deficit. For example, in 1980, off-budget expenditures were $114.3 billion. By 1989, this had increased to $210.9 billion.[23]

An example of hiding expenditures by moving them off-budget is Congress's effort in 1988 to hide $2 billion of the deficit by moving the entire Postal Service off budget. It hid a much larger chunk of the deficit by creating an off-budget enterprise, the Resolution Trust Corporation (RTC), authorized to sell $35 billion worth of revenue-backed bonds to generate funds to help clean up part of the savings and loan default mess.

Unfortunately, since RTC bonds are not as safe as bonds backed by taxes, the RTC must offer a higher interest rate to attract buyers. Estimates are that this will add about $2 billion per year in interest to the cost of salvaging America's savings and loan banks.[24] A high price to avoid telling the public the truth about the real size of the deficit.

Good Timing

This wasn't the end of the government's creative accounting. In 1989, another $4 billion was hidden by moving the military payday and farm support payments back from October 1 to September 30th. The decision was made after budget deficit estimates for 1989 were already in, and estimates for the 1990 budget were being collected. By moving the pay period back, the expended funds became part of the 1989 budget and wouldn't be included in the 1990 estimates.[25]

NOTES

[1]*Statistical Abstract of the United States* (1990), p. 324.

[2]Ibid., p. 525; tax figures based upon tax liability minus tax credits.

[3]John Schwarz, *America's Hidden Success* , p. 80.

[4]Paul Blumberg, *Inequality in an Age of Decline*, p. 93.

[5]*Statistical Abstract of the United States* (1990), p. 425; John Schwarz, *America's Hidden Success*, p. 101.

[6]John Schwarz, *America's Hidden Success,* p. 98.

[7]David Hume, *Writings on Economics* (Edinburgh: Thomas Nelson & Sons, 1955), p. 87.

[8]Stein, *Presidential Economics*, p. 251.

[9]"Research Report," *The Wilson Quarterly*, 19 (Summer 1990), p. 138.

[10]David Stockman, *The Triumph of Politics* (New York: Avon Books, 1987), p. 315.

[11]Ibid.

[12]Ibid., p. 36.

[13]Quoted in Theodore Lowi, *The End of Liberalism* (New York: W.W. Norton, 1979), p. 121.

[14]Ibid., p. 123.

[15]Jeffrey Berry, The Interest Group Society (Boston: Little, Brown, And Company, 1984), p. 183.

[16]Nelson Polsby, *Consequences of Party Reform* (Oxford: Oxford University Press, 1983), ch. 3.

[17]*How Congress Works* (Washington, D.C.: Congressional Quarterly Inc., 1983), p. 16.

[18]Paul Light, *Artful Work: The Politics of Social Security* (New York: Random House,1985), p. 102.

[19]Pechman, *Tax Reform*, p. 83.

[20]*Real World Macro*, 6th ed., p. 24.

[21]James Bennett and Thomas DiLorenzo, *Underground Government: The Off-Budget Public Sector* (Washington D.C.: Cato Institute, 1983), p. 35.

[22]Ibid., p. 38.

[23]*Budget of The United States* (1991), p. A331.

[24]John Miller, "Washington's Magic Act," Real World Macro, 7th ed., p. 20.

[25]Ibid., p. 21.

Chapter 9

Consequences of the Reagan Revolution

The Reagan administration's policies of deregulation of business, tax reduction, and tight money, known collectively as the Reagan revolution, transformed much of the economy. One consequence of these policies was the rise of monstrous budget deficits.

DEFICITS

Despite Reagan's rhetoric about reducing government spending, he did little to trim the budget. Social Security and Medicare costs rose dramatically, as did outlays for defense. With a tax increase, much of the extra spending might have been covered by additional revenue; but with two major tax cuts revenues had no chance of keeping up with expenditures. As one can see from Figure 8, in eight years Reagan nearly tripled the national debt, from about $908 billion to nearly $3 trillion dollars.

In themselves, deficits are not necessarily harmful. They can stimulate demand and contribute to economic growth. In fact, that has been one of the effects of the Reagan deficits. Nor are the deficits extraordinary by historical standards. Actually, as a percent of GNP, the growing national debt has yet to reach the high levels (63%) of the early 1950s and is about equal with the 45 percent level of the early 1960s.

CROWDING OUT

Nevertheless large deficits can cause problems. They can stimulate inflation and crowd out domestic investment in the economy. The first problem hasn't occurred because of the Fed's tight money policy. The

FIGURE 8

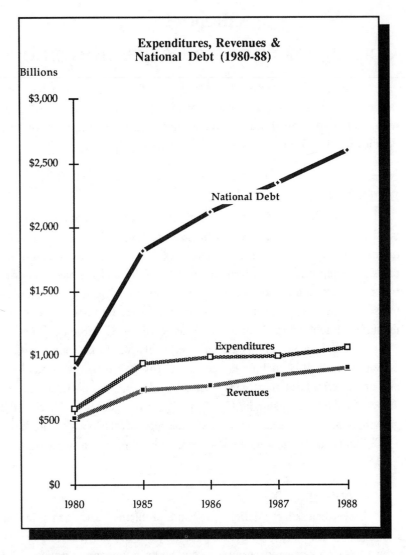

Source:*Statistical Abstract* of the United States(1990), pp. 213, 309.

Reagan deficits have not been inflationary. On the other hand, some economists believe the large deficits have crowded out a good deal of investment in the economy and consequently slowed economic growth.[1]

How might this occur? Crowding out can occur in two ways. When the deficit is financed by borrowing from private markets, and the amount involved is hundreds of billions of dollars, it can sop up a large chunk of the funds available for investment in the economy. Instead of the money going for new plants and equipment, it is used to purchase government bonds. Reduced investment in the economy can seriously hamper economic growth.

Huge deficits can crowd out investment in a more indirect way as well. Financing the deficit by borrowing from private markets, especially when the deficit is large, can raise the interest rate on bank loans. Higher interest rates discourage corporations and individuals from borrowing to finance business investment or to purchases goods.

Since the federal government has to pay for the deficit, it will always match, or come close to matching, the highest interest rate available to investors to guarantee there will be purchasers for its bonds. Banks, corporations, municipalities, and any other institution which offers interest bearing certificates, like certificates of deposit or corporate or municipal bonds, have to offer a competitive interest rate to attract customers. When the federal government markets hundreds of billions of dollars worth of bonds at high interest rates, this skews interest rates throughout financial markets. Because there is only so much money available for investment, financial institutions have to compete with the government for customers, and this means trying to match the high interest rate returned by government bonds. Of course, when banks are forced to pay high interest rates for things like certificates of deposit, they are also forced to raise interest rates on loans so they can make a profit. For instance, if banks pay 10 percent annual interest on a certificate of deposit, and charge only 9 percent interest on a loan, they suffer a 1 percent loss. To make at least a 2 percent profit they would have to raise the interest on loans to 12 percent. With loan rates so high, many potential borrowers could be priced out of the market. Some corporations might have to defer investment in new equipment or research because they can't afford the high cost of borrowed money to make the necessary investment. Ordinary individuals thinking about buying a house or car may delay their plans because high interest rates mean they can't make the monthly payments on the loans.

What all this means is that in its attempt to finance the deficit the federal government can reduce the amount of business investment that would normally occur in the economy. And this can retard economic growth.

So, in theory at least, financing large deficits could result in crowding out. However, it is difficult to determine how much crowding has occurred. For one thing, as of 1988, 13 percent of government debt was owned by foreign governments, banks, firms, and individuals. The Japanese have accounted for a large portion of this amount. In fact, in 1987, Japanese investors purchased nearly two-thirds of the government securities sold at auction.[2]

The fact that so much foreign capital has been soaking up the debt suggests the pressure on available domestic savings (money available for loans) has not been as great as the theory would indicate.[3] However, one must add that if the Fed had not kept interest rates so high (guaranteeing a high real interest for banks) whatever crowding out that did occur would not have been very severe. But by making the cost of borrowing artificially high, the Fed insured that fewer people could afford loans. So some potential borrowers were probably crowded out of the market.

FISCAL GRIDLOCK

While it remains an open question whether the Reagan deficits have crowded out a large amount of domestic investment, there is little doubt they have limited the government's ability to take on new spending. It is not only the problem that spending is already too high given existing revenue, it is that it is difficult to make cuts and free up funds for new purposes. A large part of the budget comes under what is called "relatively uncontrollable outlays". Most are expenditures which are mandated by law, things like Social Security and Medicare benefits, retirement payments for federal employees, unemployment assistance, farm price supports, etc. Some, like prior contracts for defense projects and interest payments on the national debt, are obligations for expenditures incurred in earlier years. All of these relatively uncontrollable expenditures comprise over 76 percent of federal outlays.

To reduce most of these uncontrolable expenditures, it is first necessary to change the law. For example, if Social Security or Medicare benefits are to be reduced or eligibility requirements made stiffer, Social Security legislation must be re-written. As it now stands, anyone who is sixty-five or older receives these benefits automatically, regardless of their income level. Large numbers of the elderly enjoy substantial incomes from investments or from private pensions, and many have private medical insurance. The benefits they receive from Social Security and Medicare are not actually needed. They are just frosting on the cake—extra income to finance a vacation to Europe or the Bahamas.

One could certainly make an argument that such individuals should receive no benefits or have them drastically reduced given their already high incomes. However, changing legislation that distributes benefits is not so difficult when the beneficiaries of these expenditures are politically weak, like welfare recipients. But it is extremely difficult when beneficiaries are politically powerful, like the elderly. And, as we have seen, Congress has been ill-disposed to ask constituents to make any sacrifices for the public interest. Their prime concern has been reelection. The public interest has taken a back seat.

In 1989, Social Security and Medicare payments amounted to 28.07 percent of total outlays, and defense added another 26.24 percent. Given political reality, both are difficult to reduce. The elderly are a powerful voting block, and few politicians have shown much willingness to anger them. The defense industry is equally powerful and many Congressmen would put up a bitter fight to save defense jobs in their district.

However, one large budget item exists simply because of past deficits. This is the interest paid on the national debt. In 1989 it amounted to 14.57 percent of total outlays. Without the Reagan deficits, the figure would have been much lower, perhaps no more than 5 percent of the federal budget. At this lower figure, this would mean an additional $100-$150 billion available for new spending. At the very least, it would give the government a safety margin for meeting fiscal emergencies when they arise, like the bailout for the savings and loan industry. More than that, it would mean the ability to address long delayed pressing needs like investment in the nation's decaying physical infrastructure.

Almost half of the nation's 557,600 bridges are in need of repair, and many are unsafe. Repairs also need to be made on 8,000 miles of interstate highways, not to mention the thousands of highway miles that need to be added to the system to prevent gridlock in many high population areas. In Washington state alone it is estimated that $14 billion needs to be spent to repair roads and build new ones to accommodate the increase growth in traffic. Indeed, Puget Sound has been identified as the sixth most congested area in America.[4] Sewage and water plants in many of our nation's older cities need to be repaired. Boston's water system leaks so badly it loses half its water before it ever reaches homes and businesses.

A decaying and outmoded infrastructure not only is unsightly and often dangerous, it also affects business profits. U.S. Steel has reported that the necessity of re-routing its trucks around an unsound bridge in the Pittsburgh area costs it approximately an extra $1 million per year in transportation costs.[5]

More generally, a recent report by the Federal Reserve Bank of Chicago indicates there is a direct connection between business profits and the health of America's physical infrastructure. The report states that for every 1% increase in the capital stock of America's infrastructure, there is a 2.2% increase in private profit rates.[6] It has been estimated that it would take approximately $75 billion per year to repair and upgrade America's physical infrastructure.[7]

Today, only a fraction of that amount is being spent. If it weren't for the deficit and the $165 billion in yearly interest payments it necessitates, there could be money available to meet this need.

The restraints on new spending also limit the government's ability to deal with a recession when it occurs. Government expenditures naturally go up during a recession. More money has to be spent on unemployment and welfare checks, and additional funds have to be set aside for more food stamps. If the recession is severe, government may need to increase spending generally to help stimulate aggregate demand to get the economy going again. All of this proves difficult when the budget is already in deficit because of insufficient revenue to cover the costs of existing programs. In fact the pressures are all in the opposite direction— to hold down expenses and avoid any new spending. A reticence to take on new spending might very well prolong a recession and the misery associated with it.

Of course, this problem would diminish if something was done to reduce the deficit. Since politicians have been unwilling to reduce expenditures, the only option is to raise revenue through high taxes. The trouble is that the politicians may have waited too long. Recessions are a rather frequent occurrence in the American economy. It seems nearly impossible to avoid one for very long. One is therefore about due. If this is so, it would be tempting fate to raise taxes at this late date. A tax increase would dampen demand and perhaps nudge the economy into a premature recession, or if one has aleady occurred it could seriously prolong it. Such thoughts have no doubt occurred to the President and his advisors. They have also likely crossed the mind of some Congressmen. For this reason, if tax increases occur they will likely be too small to significantly reduce the deficit for some time.

BALANCE OF TRADE

Another, more serious, consequence of large deficits, coupled with artificially high interest rates, has been the effect on the U.S. balance of trade (see Figure 9). The U.S. experienced its first trade deficit in the 20th century in 1971. That year we bought more from foreigners than we

FIGURE 9

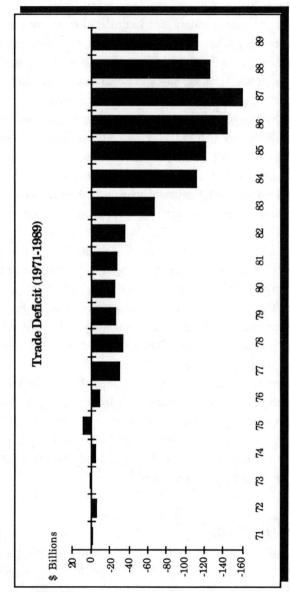

Trade Deficit (1971-1989)

Source: *Real World Macro*, 7th ed., p. 92.

sold to them. It was the first sign that America had lost some of its competitive edge in international markets. The trade deficit was small, however, and did not increase appreciably until 1977 when it jumped from $9.1 to $31.1 billion. The next big jump occurred in 1983 when the trade deficit rose to $67.1 billion.

This quantum leap in the trade deficit was mostly the result of a strengthening of the dollar. Inflation that year dropped from 6.1 to 3.2 percent. The dollar was now worth more than before, not only at home but abroad where exchange rates reflected a sudden tilt in favor of the dollar.

The value of the dollar was further enhanced by continuing high interest rates and a growing deficit that had to be financed at those high rates. This attracted foreign capital, resulting in an increase in demand of dollar dominated financial instruments (government bonds). Exchange rates reflected this demand for the dollar. The dollar was now worth more vis-a-vis foreign currencies. This meant it could buy more than before in Europe and Japan. It also meant that foreigners purchasing American goods had to pay more marks or yen for them than before. The good news was that foreign goods became less expensive for Americans. The bad news was that American goods also became more expensive to foreigners. Orders for our exports declined, while imports soared.

The difficulty was not just that American firms were losing sales abroad, they were being edged out of foreign markets. The Japanese were able to sell cheaper cars to Europe and capture a larger share of the market. American steel was edged out by French steel, and machine tools produced in America could not compete with much lower priced machine tools produced in West Germany. Manufacturing wasn't the only victim. By 1983, American grain farmers lost more than a third of the global market to foreign competitors.[8]

Once competitors capture a market it is difficult to dislodge them. Loyalty to sellers and their products form and deepen. Buyers agree to sign long-term contracts. American manufacturing, mining and agriculture were devastated, not only abroad but at home as well. Because of the increase in the purchase of imported goods, foreign competitors were also increasing their share of American markets.

For instance, by 1987 the U.S. steel industry was near collapse. Plants were closed to cut costs, thousands of steel workers were laid off, and production of steel declined precipitously. American steel simply couldn't compete with steel made in Brazil, South Korea, Argentina and Mexico. Foreign instead of American steel was being used to make American automobiles, girders and pipes.

Even the Defense Department was contributing to the demise of American steel. I recently spent a hot Saturday afternoon at Fairchild Air Force Base to watch my brother play in a baseball game sponsored by the Special Olympics. Between innings I joined the thirsty crowd at the water fountain. When it was my turn, I noticed new pipe had been installed in the fountain. The name of the manufacturer was stenciled on the side in black paint. It read: "Dongguk Heavy Industry." Dongguk is a city on the outskirts of Seoul. The pipe had been manufactured in South Korea. It was gratifying to realize Fairchild was watching its pennies and purchasing the cheapest pipe it could find. But it was also a sad commentary on the dismal state of the American steel industry.

To undo all of this requires time, and highly competitive prices. For some companies, no amount of time or a drastic devaluation of the dollar would be enough to help. Certainly this was true for those which had given up and closed their factories. It was also true for failing companies that had abandoned America and moved their factories off shore, becoming part of the problem rather than part of the solution. Now they produced imports for America rather than exports for abroad.

By 1985, pressures for devaluing the dollar forced the government to act. In September of that year, the U.S. persuaded West Germany, Japan, France and Britain to direct their central banks to sell dollars, forcing exchange rates to rise vis-a-vis the dollar. Within a year, the dollar declined by 33 percent against ten other leading currencies. But even with a devalued dollar, the trade deficit persisted.

As one can see from Figure 9, it wasn't until 1988 that some light appeared at the end of the tunnel. That year U.S. exports jumped by 27 percent, shaving $33 billion off of the trade deficit. The trade deficit declined again in 1989, down by nearly $47 billion from the 1987 high of $160.3 billion. Agriculture had rebounded, and the aircraft industry was building a hefty surplus in foreign sales. But manufacturing, especially in autos and steel, was still in deficit with no end in sight. While there has been an improvement in the general trade picture, it remains to be seen whether the U.S. will be able to achieve a trade surplus any time in the near future.

THE SELLING OF AMERICA

The devaluation of the dollar had another consequence. It made assets in the U.S. cheap for foreign buyers whose currency suddenly skyrocketed in value compared to the dollar. Within a year the Japanese discovered that they could purchase twice as much in America for the same amount of yen as they could before the devaluation. In fact, the dollar value of all the real estate in Tokyo alone ($7.7 trillion) was large enough to buy all the land in the U.S., plus all the companies listed on the New York Stock Exchange. And a good deal of that capital worth was finding its way into financial markets. Many home owners in Japan discovered that the value of their property was so high hardly anyone could afford to purchase it. They were sitting on an extremely valuable asset but were unable to realize any financial benefit from it. A large number discovered a way around this impasse. They mortgaged their homes and used the money to invest in financial markets. Suddenly, Japan was flush with capital seeking outlets for investment. Because they had suddenly become so inexpensive, American assets became a prime target for these investment funds.

Not only the Japanese but many other foreigners began a buying spree in the U.S. The largest investments came from Britain, but a good deal of that amount actually came from oil rich Arab states routing money through British investment firms into the U.S. From whatever source, total foreign investment in the American economy is quite impressive.

FIGURE 10

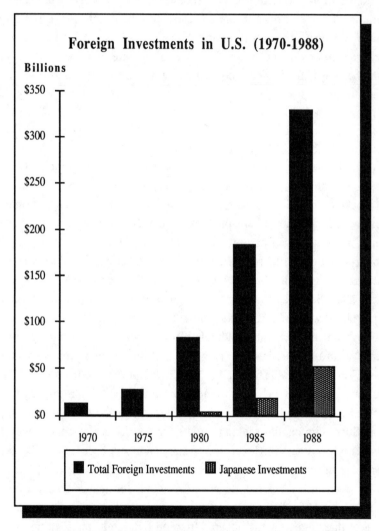

Source: *Statistical Abstract of the United States (1990)*, p. 794. Figures represent ownership of 25% or more of U.S. asset.

For example, In 1985, foreign investment in the U.S. stood at $184 billion. This included stock in companies, commercial property, companies and land—various assets in which foreigners owned more than 25 percent. By 1988, it had grown to $329 billion.[9]

Twelve percent of America's manufacturing base is now in foreign hands. Also, by 1988, foreigners had acquired ownership of 46 percent of the commercial real estate in downtown Los Angeles, nearly as much in Houston, 32 percent of Minneapolis' commercial property and 21 percent of Manhattan's. Foreigners used $80 billion to take over major U.S. corporations. The British acquired Hilton International and Holiday Inns as well as Smith & Wesson and Brooks Brothers. The West Germans now own Ball Park Franks and French's mustard. The Japanese bought the Dunes Hotel in Los Vegas, and Tiffany and the Algonquin hotel in New York city, and the CBS record company. The Australians snapped up United Artists and Twentieth Century-Fox.[10] Let's not forget banking. In 1988, twenty percent of bank assets in America were also foreign owned, mostly by Japan.[11]

One difficulty with so many companies being owned by foreigners is that up to 80 percent of profits are siphoned off and sent home. That is income that could have been spent or invested in the U.S. Also foreign owned companies import more goods, often parts or material from the parent company back home, than American owned firms. Indeed, in 1986, the imports of foreign owned companies accounted for about half of that year's trade deficit.[12]

REDISTRIBUTION OF INCOME

THE BAD 70S

The decade of the 1970s was a tough one for most American wage earners. Inflation and taxes eroded their incomes. The influx of the baby boomers into the labor market created an over supply of workers and depressed wages. Except for workers in strong unions, many blue collar employees had trouble keeping up with inflation. For example, a machine

FIGURE 11

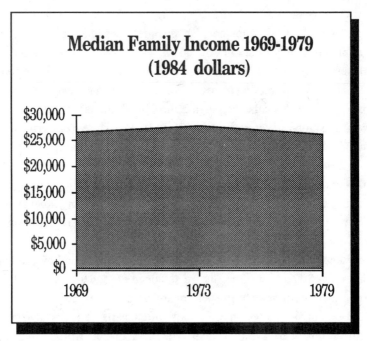

Source: Frank Levy, *Dollars and Dreams*, ch. 4.

operator saw his real income decline 0.9 percent between 1969 and 1979. The real income of police and firemen dropped 10.1 percent. Food workers lost 8.1 percent.

Even white collar workers faced special difficulties. The competition for professional jobs became intense. A higher percentage of young people were earning college degrees than ever before. In 1959, only 12 percent of white males between 25 and 29 graduated from college. By 1979, that figure had jumped to 27 percent. With so many college trained people competing for professional jobs, professional incomes declined.

There were exceptions. In the 1970s doctors and dentists enjoyed a modest increase of 3.2 percent in real income. People in management did even better with a whopping 20.2 percent rise in real income. But for nearly everyone else from engineers, lawyers, social workers, salesmen and technicians, real incomes declined over the decade.[13]

Lumping everyone in together, and measured in 1984 dollars, median family income was actually slightly lower in 1979 than it was in 1969 (see Figure 11). This is a remarkable figure since the 70s was the decade when many families had two wage earners. Yet, even with both the husband and wife working, median family income still declined.

No wonder people wanted to believe in Reagan's supply-side magic. Unfortunately, most families didn't benefit from the Reagan revolution. Median family income continued to decline for most of Reagan's two terms. Only by 1987 did it rise to match in real dollar terms what it had been way back in 1973. Individual workers, rather than families, didn't even do that well. Inflation adjusted average weekly income for American workers was actually $54 lower in 1987 than it was in 1972, and $6 dollars lower than in 1980.[14]

One way people adjusted to declining real income during the Reagan era was to forestall a slide in their standard of living by going heavily into debt. Credit markets have adjusted to this response by making it easier for consumers to bear higher debt burdens. Many loans are now pegged to longer terms, five or seven years compared to the two or three year loans of the 1970s. This keeps monthly payments lower so families can manage higher debt. Just how much higher is the debt load? In 1980, average household debt stood at about 75 percent of yearly earnings. By 1988 it had climbed to 93.9 percent—the highest since the end of the Second World War.[15]

THE PRIVILEGED MINORITY
Not everyone did poorly, though. A small segment of America did extremely well. A brief glance at the gains and losses in family income

FIGURE 12

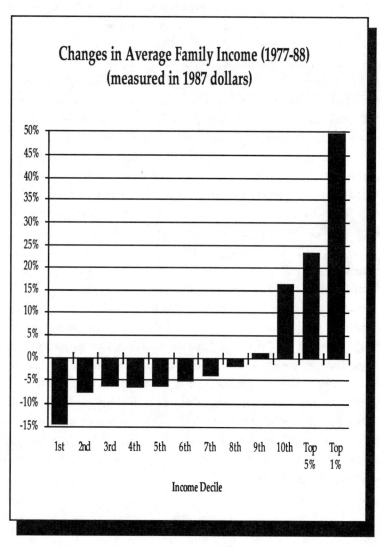

Source: Kevin Phillips, *The Politics of Rich and Poor*, p. 17.

between 1977-1988 (Figure 12) reveals that the top 10 percent enjoyed a 16 percent increase in income. The income decile just below them only gained 1 percent, while everyone else lost income. Actually, families at the very top of the income strata did the best. The top 5 percent saw their income increase by a hefty 23.4 percent; and the top 1 percent enjoyed a whopping 49.8 percent increase in income.

DEFICITS AND JUNK

How did this happen? Financing the deficit accounts for part of the change. Because the Fed kept interest rates so high, government bonds offered substantial returns to those who could afford to purchase them. In fact, people at the top 20 percent of the income ladder purchased about 80 percent of all these bonds and received high interest income from them. In 1988, the interest payment on the national debt was $210 billion for that year. This was nearly half of all the federal income tax dollars collected from ordinary wage earners. In effect, the interest payment was a huge transfer of income from average Americans to the highest income earners in America.[16]

The Reagan administration's emphasis on deregulation also helped to increase the incomes of the already well-to-do. Bank deregulation allowed banks to make speculative investments and loans, and for a while some reaped enormous profits. Only later would it become clear that deregulation was leading the banking community, and especially the savings and loan banks, to ultimate ruin. But meanwhile there were fortunes to be made—not only in banking but in the growing merger movement taking place in corporate America. The number of mergers and acquisitions grew from 1,500 in 1980 to a high of 4,381 in 1986. The values involved were large, rising from a mere $33 billion in 1980 to $227 billion in 1988 (Figure 13).

The middlemen, lawyers and stockbrokers who arranged mergers, acquisitions and hostile takeovers, earned bloated fees for their services. In particular, the emergence of the junk bond market was a wonderful windfall to such middlemen.

FIGURE 13

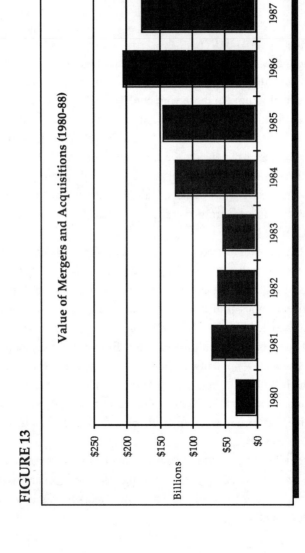

Value of Mergers and Acquisitions (1980-88)

Source: *Statistical Abstract of the United States (1990),* p. 534.

A corporate bond is debt, a loan from the purchaser of the bond to the corporation who sells it. Like any loan it pays interest, usually every six months. All things equal, the higher the interest paid, the more attractive the bond. But all things aren't always equal. One has to also take into consideration the ability of the corporation to meet interest payments on its bonds. This is the risk component. If a corporation has little debt and enjoys substantial earnings, its ability to meet bond obligations is excellent. If it already has a lot of debt, or its earnings are low, then it could be a bad risk. Prior to the 1980s, junk bonds were what their name implies. They were very risky investments. The likelihood that the corporations issuing them could actually pay them off was low. Bond rating agencies like Moody and Standard and Poor informed potential buyers whether bonds were top rated or junk, the junk category being bonds whose risk factor was so high they were not considered investment quality.

Because they were rated so low, there was not a large market for junk bonds. If a corporation couldn't get a high rating for a bond issue, it simply didn't bother issuing it. Junk just didn't sell. In the early 1970s, a Wall Street investment firm, Drexel Burnham Lambert, began to specialize in marketing junk bonds. It convinced many investors that some junk bonds were really a good bargain. Because they had such low ratings, junk bonds offered much higher than average interest rates to attract nervous customers. And Drexel explained to its customers that a number of the bonds were not as risky as the bond raters claimed. By 1976, junk bonds had become a $15 billion market.

However, it wasn't until the mid-1980s when the merger and acquisition craze caught on that junk bonds really came into their own. Drexel realized that junk bonds could be used by hungry corporations to raise the capital necessary to take over other corporations. It was simple. Sell the junk bonds and use the proceeds to buy up a controlling share of the target corporation's stock. Then, for all practical purposes, you owned it. Part of the secret to making the bonds marketable was to let it be known that a takeover attempt was in the offing. Even if the corporation attempting the takeover had neither the revenue nor the assets to ever pay the interest on its junk bonds, if the takeover proved successful it could sell off large chunks of the target corporation and raise the necessary cash to make the interest payments. It took only a few successful junk bond financed take-overs to get the ball rolling. Investors scrambled to purchase high interest takeover junk bonds.

Many corporations fearing an imminent takeover by this means, employed a similar technique to prevent it. The most direct approach was to buy up their own stock so no one else could get their hands on it. And an easy way to get the capital for these buy-backs was to sell junk bonds. The other nice thing about this maneuver is that it so burdened a company with debt it was no longer an attractive target for takeover. During the 1980s, corporations retired about $500 billion of their stock, replacing it with about $1 trillion in debt, a good deal of it junk bond debt. The reason the debt was higher than the stock value was the hefty interest payments corporations had to pay to holders of their junk. The extent of this debt is highlighted by the fact that, in 1989, U.S. corporations paid more in interest on their debt than they earned in after-tax profit.[17]

By 1989, junk bonds had become a $200 billion market. Firms like Drexel that managed junk bond sales charged 3 percent for the service, 300 percent higher than the normal fee for handling top rated corporate stocks and bonds. This translated into incredible salaries for employees of firms like Drexel specializing in the junk bond market. One Drexel employee, Michael Milken, earned $550 million in just one year.[18]

The trouble with all of the takeovers and debt financed stock purchases by panicked companies trying to prevent them is that it did almost nothing to improve the efficiency of businesses or increase the output of goods and services. All that happened was that ownership of companies changed hands. Mostly what it did was generate a massive amount of debt, force companies to sell off their most productive assets to pay for it, and line the pockets of the middlemen who arranged all the deals and, for a time, the bank accounts of investors who gobbled up the high interest bearing junk bonds. Lots of money was made by already wealthy people. Nothing substantial was gained by the economy.

Often, a great deal was lost. An example will drive this point home. American Sign & Indicator Corporation was a local success story for Spokane, Washington. Founded by Luke and Charles Williams in 1951, the company marketed bank signs that flash the time and temperature. From sales in Spokane (Seattle National Bank at Howard and Riverside was the first bank to display such a sign) to banks across the state, then to sales to banks in other states, American Sign established a national, and later an international market for its products which eventually included electronic scoreboards for sports arenas such as the Pontiac Silverdome and Madison Square Garden and electric board advertising for businesses. By 1979, the company employed 750 people, and had established a sign leasing program worth over $90 million.

Then, in 1983, American Sign became a victim of the buyout craze. It was purchased for $20 million by Brae Corporation, a San Francisco based company. It was a good deal for Brae which immediately turned around and sold off the lease program of American Sign for $97 million. With this lucrative part of the company gone, Brae had little interest in what remained. It sold American Sign for $1, took a tax loss and earned $7.8 million in tax benefits. In all, for a mere $20 million investment, Brae had dismantled American Sign and sold its parts for a total return of $104.8 million.

Meanwhile, the ownership of American Sign passed from one company to another, each headquartered in another state and only interested in maximizing profits for the parent company rather than for American Sign or for Spokane. By 1990, employment in American sign had declined to under 200 and there was talk by its parent company, Winko-Matic Signal of Georgia, to reduce American Sign to a subsidiary manufacturing plant with as few as 30 employees. If this plan goes through, American Sign will no longer employ a research staff of top flight engineers and computer programmers who pioneered the innovative electric sign technology that originally put the company on the map.[19]

Takeovers and buyouts may have been profitable for some companies, but for many others, and the cities and towns dependent on them for jobs, the picture has been less bright.

The Reagan administration could have interceded and slowed down the pace of mergers and acquisitions or even reversed events. But Reagan was against the regulation of business, and directed the Justice Department to refrain from investigating the takeovers for potential anti-trust violations. The consequences of this failure to regulate is beginning to be felt in the 1990s. Some of the corporations that burdened themselves with junk bond debt have already gone under, unable to meet the interest payments. In 1989, 14 companies defaulted on $3 billion worth of junk bonds. Many other debt burdened corporations are teetering toward collapse.

CEO COMPENSATION

During the Reagan years the incomes of corporate executives rose sharply. Often this occurred without any economic justification. Millions of blue-collar employees had been laid off. Those who were left were forced to pick up the slack of their unemployed brethren. And they did. Factory floor productivity rose by about 3 percent per year. Unfortunately the overall productivity of these firms was way below this figure. Why? Well, at the same time blue-collar workers were being laid off, more white-collar workers were being hired, an increase of 21 percent between 1979 to 1985.[20] The reason total productivity was below the 3 percent level of floor workers was that the swollen white-collar bureaucracy of many firms was grossly inefficient. If anyone should have received increases in pay it should have been the blue-collar workers, not the corporate executives.

But the Fed's tight money policy had nearly broken the unions, and they were not in a good position to protest. Then there was the new supply-side ideology with a clear moral: "to get the rich moving, give them money. For the poor, there was an appropriate corollary. One took money and benefits away from them for their own good, on the ground ... that the poor need the spur of their poverty in order to escape from it."[21]

According to this reasoning, it was the rich who performed all the economic magic, and it was they who should be rewarded to spur them on to even greater feats of entrepreneurial prestidigitation. Thus, it was corporate executives rather than workers who deserved hefty wage increases because increasing the wages of factory workers would not really benefit the economy; workers aren't entrepreneurs, they don't make the economy grow.

Between 1983 and 1987, the salaries of top corporate officers jumped by 56.8 percent. Lower management also registered gains—a 32.6 increase in salary. In 1987, the average compensation for the CEOs (Chief Executive Officers) of the nations largest 339 corporations was $1.8 million. A year later it stood at $2.02 million.

The discrepancy between the salaries of top executives and factory floor workers widened dramatically during the Reagan years. In 1979, CEOs earned 29 times the income of average manufacturing worker. In 1985 this jumped to 40, and in 1988 it climbed to 93 times greater than the average factory worker's earnings.[22]

By the various means described above, the top 5 percent of Americans increased their share of the nation's income by about 4 percent. That means in a $4 trillion economy a transfer of $160 billion per year from average Americans to the super rich. To make this more concrete, it means 32 million wage earners giving up $5,000 per year to support the income gains of the top 5 percent.[23]

No wonder the Reagan era became the golden age of millionaires. In 1981 there were 600,000 millionaires in America. In 1988 that number rose to 1,500,000. Before 1981, there were only a handful of Americans worth $10 million or more; by 1988 there were 100,000. While there were almost none at the beginning of the decade, by 1988 there were 1,200 people worth over $100 million   There were no billionaires before 1981. By 1988 there were fifty-one.[24]

FIGURE 14

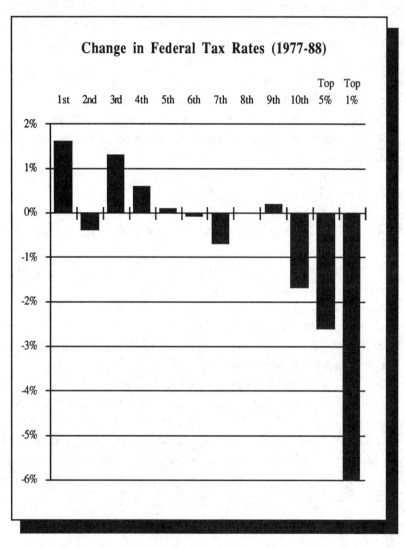

Source: Kevin Phillips, *The Politics of Rich and Poor*, p. 83.

TAXES

Tax reform also benefited the rich more than the average American. High income earners paid a smaller percentage of what they earned in taxes. In 1980, people with high income were taxed at a 70 percent rate. This dropped to 50 percent in 1981 and down to 28 percent in 1988. The tax on capital gains (proceeds from the sale of property and other assets) also declined and then was treated as ordinary income as was income from interest.

At first blush it would seem that everyone benefited, rich and poor alike. True, the income tax liability of very poor people nearly disappeared. Most paid no income tax at all. The middle class also gained, averaging about a 9 percent decline in income taxes.

On the other hand, while the income tax was being lowered for everyone, the Social Security tax was being increased; and it affected lower and middle income people more than those with high incomes. Social Security taxes increased from 6.05 percent of wages in 1978 to 6.7 percent in 1983, 7.5 percent in 1985, and 7.51 percent in 1988. Since Social Security taxes are levied on only the first $35,000 of earnings, individuals with very high earnings pay a smaller proportion of their income for this tax. Someone earning $200,000 in 1988 would have had a combined tax liability for income and Social Security taxes of about 29.3 percent, while a person with income of $50,000 would have a combined liability of about 33.3 percent. Indeed, when one compares the total federal tax liability of different income groups (Figure 14), it becomes clear that high income Americans fared much better than low and middle income Americans during the Reagan era.

Thus, not only did the rich become much richer, they were able to keep a larger portion of what they earned while most other Americans who didn't share in the income bonanza had a higher percentage of their income taxed away.

FUTURE REVOLT?

It is interesting to note that Kevin Phillips, the author and Republican activist who accurately predicted in his 1967 book, *The Emerging Republican Majority*, that the Republicans would soon dominate American politics, nevertheless argues in his most recent book, *The Politics of Rich and Poor*, that the excesses of the Reagan era will likely result in their loss of political ascendancy. He sees historical parallels which he believes confirms this prediction.

Phillips identifies three periods of Republican ascendancy. The first was the period of post Civil War economic expansion known as the Gilded Age; the second period in the 1920s was another time of economic expansion, dubbed by historians as the Roaring Twenties. The most recent period of Republican ascendancy is the Reagan era. In each period, the Republicans supported tight money, low taxes, and unregulated markets. And in each period, wealth and income was shifted upward.

Two events signalled the end of the first two periods. First, an economic downturn: for the Gilded Age it ws the depression of 1893-1897; and, for the Roaring Twenties, it was the Great Depression. The second event was political upheaval directed against the unequal distribution of wealth and income and the excesses of unfettered capitalism. In both instances, Phillips argues, the Republicans lost their political ascendancy and the Democrats made political gains.

He suggests the same thing might happen again. Should there be a major recession, voter defection from the Republicans might be great, and the demand arise for more regulation of the economy, more concern for economic losers, and higher taxes for the wealthy. Indeed, he already sees signs pointing in that direction. A 1987 poll by the National Opinion Research center revealed that 59 percent of Americans felt "the wealthy weren't taxed enough, and in 1989 slightly more than 50 percent of those polled by the Center said the government should reconsider raising taxes for wealthy individuals, or making direct payments to the poor, to reduce the income gap between the haves and have-nots."[25]

Alas, the historical record is not that straightforward. Take the Gilded Age. To be sure, the Republicans supported tight money. During the Civil War, in addition to heavy borrowing, the government printed money (greenbacks) to help pay for expenses. They were backed by neither gold nor silver. This increased the money supply and caused high inflation. The inflation especially hurt banks and financiers because it depressed their real earnings (interest adjusted for inflation). Most were staunch Republicans and urged their party to return to a hard money policy. In 1875, Congress passed the Specie Resumption Act which retired the greenbacks from circulation and put the nation on a gold standard. The money supply contracted and the money interests enjoyed a dramatic increase in income.

During this same period, immigration increased expanding the total supply of workers and, invariably depressing wages. Low wages increased the profits of industrial corporations. It was also a time of unfettered economic expansion and the growing concentration of business. Not only bankers and financiers, but the full range of capitalists grew richer, while ordinary workers and farmers struggled to survive.

Not only did the wealthy class enjoy the support of government, they also benefited from the support of religion. Many prominent clergymen espoused what would come to be known as the Gospel of Wealth, a creed which emphasized the moral superiority of the wealthy which, it was argued, justified class distinctions. Close upon its heels came Social Darwinism which viewed the economy on analogy with wild nature where only the fittest survive. Of course, the capitalist were the fittest. The economic losers—paupers and workers living at subsistence wages—were the unfit. According to the doctrine, the poor and poorly paid deserved what they got. If they were more fit, they would have gotten more. And it was best for the human race that the fittest prospered and passed on their genes while the unfit perished from the earth. The wealthy now had both God and science on their side to justify the privileges they enjoyed.

As Phillips points out, such hardheartedness, and the suffering and hardship it ignored, did eventually result in voter backlash. Indeed, protests began to increase, not only among populist politicians but also in literature. Today, Frank Baum's *Wonderful Wizard of Oz* is viewed as a delightful fairy tail, but when it was published (1890) it was rightly understood by many as a thinly veiled attack on the eastern money interests. It was the decent midwestern farm values of Auntie Em, and the good heart of the tin woodsman, pitted against the wicked witch of the east (bankers). The yellow brick road (gold) led to OZ (for gold ounces) where the wizard representing the establishment elite, was eventually unmasked as a fraud.

The depression of 1893-1897 increased the hardship for those already suffering. Unemployment eventually reached 20 percent. Food prices declined further depressing the already beleaguered farm economy. A third party was formed, the Populists, and the demand arose among Populist politicians for cheap money, if not a return to greenbacks at least a move to a silver rather than a gold standard. Silver mines were delivering record amounts of the mineral, guaranteeing a constantly growing money supply; it would mean an end to tight money.

The Populists nominated William Jennings Bryan for their candidate for the 1896 Presidential election. But so did the Democrats. It was a strange sight, two parties running the same man. Being the Democratic candidate didn't help Bryan. The Democrats had won the Presidency in 1892, and Grover Cleveland was blamed for the depression. The Democrats were repudiated at the polls. Bryan was defeated by the Republican candidate, William McKinley.

Perhaps things would have turned out differently if a Republican President had been in office during the depression. As it turned out, the Republicans were able to portray themselves as the party of prosperity, the party that would end the depression.

After Bryan's defeat, the Populist movement collapsed and protest subsided. And the issue of easy money receded into the background. The economy recovered after McKinley took office, partly as a result of the discovery of huge deposits of gold in the Alaskan Klondike. The money supply increased sharply. There was no need for a silver standard to soften hard money.

The Republicans controlled the Presidency until 1912, and then were again in power from 1920 until 1932. During The Roaring Twenties, the rich again got richer, wages remained low, and hard money was the rule. It took the Great Depression to finally bring an end to a very long period of Republican ascendancy.

The difficulty with Phillips' thesis is that it is hard to tell whether the Reagan era is like the Gilded Age or the Roaring Twenties. If it is like the Gilded Age, there is no reason to believe the Republicans will lose their grip on power. Indeed, there is little evidence that those most hurt by capitalist excesses will protest at all. As Phillips himself admits, only 50 percent of the eligible electorate voted in the 1988 Presidential election. Moreover, about fifty percent of the votes cast in the election came from the richest 40 percent of the voters, enough to swing almost any election in their favor. Poor people tend not to vote. No one is sure why, but many analysts believe it is because they have given up and feel the political system no longer responds to their needs. If people who have suffered the most from the Reagan revolution refuse to become involved in politics, to voice their protest at the ballot box, what is the likelihood things will change? Will thirty-six years have to pass, as it did after the 1896 election, and the economy collapse, before voters will ask for a major change?

BANKING CRISIS

Not only did Reaganomics contribute to fiscal gridlock, lost foreign markets, the selling of America, and a dramatic upward redistribution of income, with Congressional aid it also set the stage for the financial collapse of America's savings and loan industry.

Historically, there have been two kinds of banks in America: commercial banks primarily serving corporate banking needs, and savings banks, called thrifts, serving the banking needs of ordinary citizens.

Prior to 1932, the thrifts were of two kinds: mutual savings banks and building and loan associations. Mutual savings banks are depositor owned and controlled. People who have savings in these banks have a say how they are run. The first mutual savings bank, Provident Institution for Savings of Boston, was established in 1816. Two others, in Philadelphia and New York, soon followed. Because their depositors wanted to protect their life savings, mutual savings banks were careful with their investments, usually purchasing government and municipal bonds—the safest of all investments. Eventually, mutual savings banks became the banks of America's immigrants, and their deposits invested in government bonds helped finance many of the public works project of cities and states throughout the country.

The second type of savings bank was the building and loan association. Originally begun in the 1840s, the savings and loan associations were the banks of the middle class, associations for the deposit of savings to be used for the eventual purchase of a home. Over time, the building and loan banks began operating like ordinary savings banks, taking in deposits from one group of people, and making home loans to others. By the turn of the century, the building and loan associations had become so successful their assets surpassed those of the mutual savings banks.[26] The building and loan associations were transformed into a national system of savings and loan banks (S&Ls) by New Deal Banking legislation. And it is this same savings and loan industry that is now on the verge of collapse.

NEW DEAL LEGISLATION

Ironically, the S&L crisis of the 1980s was partially the result of legislation to correct an earlier crisis in American banking. This earlier crisis occurred during the Great Depression. In 1933, bank loans were down by 59 percent. Many banks suffered runs and were unable to repay depositors and had to close. To shore up confidence in the banking system, the Emergency Bank Act of 1933 created the Federal Deposit Insurance Corporation (FDIC) which insured bank deposits for up to $2,500. That same year, the Home Owner's Loan Corporation Act created a national system of savings and loan banks. Unlike mutual savings banks, which are depositor owned and primarily serve the savings needs of their depositors, and commercial banks which make loans to corporations, the savings and loan banks are for working people. Like the mutual savings banks the S&Ls were meant to be a safe harbor for the working man's savings, and like the building and loan associations they were supposed to be a major source of housing loans, but now the working as well as the middle class would benefit.

To make them attractive to depositors, savings and loan banks were allowed by law to offer a higher interest on deposits for non-corporate customers (1/2 a percent higher) than commercial banks. There was a price for this favoritism. Unlike commercial banks, S&Ls were not allowed to offer checking accounts to customers. On the other hand, their deposits were as safe as those in commercial banks. This was guaranteed by a separate institution, the Savings and Loan Insurance Corporation (FSLIC), established to insure deposits in S&Ls up to $2,500.

At the time everyone thought insured deposits was a great idea. No one imagined it might sow the seeds of disaster fifty years later.

INFLATION AND THE S&LS

The S&Ls flourished after the Second World War. The demand for home loans remained strong, and inflation was low, guaranteeing high real interest for banks holding long term fixed-rate mortgages. Then inflation began to surge in the late 1960s. By the early 1970s, S&Ls started losing money. They had billions invested in long term loans at modest interest rates, rates that were being eroded by inflation. For example, a 3 percent mortgage during a period of 5 percent inflation resulted in a negative 2 percent return on the investment.

On top of this, S&Ls were losing depositors. Restricted by law to offering only 5.5 percent interest on deposits, when inflation climbed above this level, depositors began withdrawing their money from S&L savings accounts and placing them in NOW and money market accounts. In one month nearly $2 billion was bled from savings and loan banks. In another month the figure rose to $5 billion. By 1979, money market funds had accumulated $250 billion in assets, about equal to what the S&Ls had accumulated during their entire existence.

NOW AND MONEY MARKETS

A NOW account (Negotiated Order of Withdrawal) is an interest bearing checking account. It was invented by commercial banks in 1972. Many people figured the new checking accounts were a good deal. The interest on NOW accounts wasn't high, but it sure beat no interest at all, plus a service charge, which was typical of ordinary checking accounts.

Money market accounts were also popular. Before 1972, only the corporate customers of commercial banks could earn exceptionally high interest on savings. This was because the commercial banks could offer any interest rate they wanted to corporate customers. Prior to 1972, this didn't affect the S&Ls. Their customers weren't corporations, so they couldn't take advantage of this policy. Things changed after 1972, for in that year investment houses began making huge deposits in commercial banks. Because the investors were corporations, they were able to earn high interest on these deposits. Nothing new here. But what was new was that they turned around and sold shares in these deposits to ordinary people, deducting a small percent of the interest earned as a service charge and passing the rest of the high interest on to the shareholders. In effect, the investment houses discovered a way to allow ordinary people to enjoy the same high interest as corporate savers. It was an easy way for small savers to attempt to beat inflation.

CONGRESS TO THE RESCUE

With inflation destroying their earnings and NOW and money market accounts depriving them of customers, the S&Ls asked Congress for help. It was forthcoming. In 1978, Congress authorized S&Ls to offer customers money market accounts. Unfortunately, because they had lost so many depositors the S&Ls were low on funds and had to borrow from commercial banks. The difference between the interest they paid the commercial banks and the interest they earned from their money market accounts was therefore very small. The S&Ls needed additional help to survive.

In 1980, Congress passed the Deregulation and Monetary Control Act. The Act raised insured deposits covered by both the FDIC and FSLIC from $40,000 to $100,000, dramatically increasing the government's liability for deposited funds in America's banks.

However, this didn't help S&Ls much. That year they lost $4 billion. New legislation in 1982 offered more aid. The Garn-St Germain Depository Institutions Decontrol Act allowed S&Ls to invest in anything they wanted. They were no longer required to invest only in real estate mortgages.

Then, in 1983, the Federal Home Loan Bank Board announced that the S&Ls could finance 100 percent of real estate loans. Previously, they were limited to financing 80 percent of a home or property's appraised value. Investors or contractors seeking funds to finance home construction had to come up with the other 20 percent. That 20 percent acted as a restraint. Since investors had to put up some of their own money, they had an incentive to only borrow funds for good investments. Now that restraint had vanished. They could borrow the entire amount. None of their own money was involved.

It was an invitation to reckless speculation in real estate. If an investment didn't pan out, the bank was left holding the bag. For their part, banks weren't terribly worried either because funds for loans came from insured deposits. If a loan went sour, the government had to cover the lost deposit. It was insured after all. Between 1983 and 1986, savings and loan real estate loans doubled from $74 to $140 billion, many in highly speculative deals.

The original intention behind insured deposits was to instill confidence in banks, to let the public know they were safe places to deposit their money. Now, instead of making banks safe, insured deposits encouraged risky ventures.

But the S&Ls weren't just making real estate loans. Garn-St. Germain allowed them to invest in anything they wanted. To increase their revenues as quickly as possible and make up for all the money lost on low interest mortgages depreciated by inflation, many S&Ls began investing in high yield junk bonds to the tune of about $100 billion.

ABUSES AND CORRUPTION

The relaxation of banking regulations invited abuses. First, Garn-St Germain had reduced the net worth requirement for opening an S&L. For as little as $3 million an investor could become a savings and loan banker. Then, in 1983, S&Ls were permitted to charge a special fee (up to 6 percent of a loan amount) for putting together a loan for real estate development or acquisition. Clever investors saw an opening to make a fast buck. Open an S&L for a $3 million investment, accumulate $100 million in deposits, then lend the whole amount out to speculators with a 6 percent origination of loan fee. That's a $6 million return on a $3 million investment. If the investment went bad, the government would have to pick up the tab because it was all based on insured deposits. Speculators rushed into banking with predictable results.

Then there was old fashioned corruption. The Reagan administration was emphasizing the decontrol of business, including banks. Bank regulators saw their staff reduced. Accounting rules were relaxed. In the new environment it was easy to cheat and not get caught. Bank officials loaned millions to family members, padded their salaries, and used bank funds for pleasure trips and executive jets. Never one to overlook an opportunity to defraud depositors, the unofficial king of S&L sleeze, Texas banker Don Dixon, arranged loans to friends who used the funds to pay Dixon's living expenses. Of course, Dixon never expected the loans to be paid off. It was simply a clever way to funnel bank funds into his own pocket or, in the case of one of these loans, to pay the rent on Dixon's California beach house.[27]

Officials at the Federal Home Loan Bank Board charged with overseeing the savings and loan industry suspected things were going wrong and asked for more staff to conduct audits of S&Ls suspected of mismanagement and fraud. But they were told none would be supplied. Indeed, the official who made the request, was told he "was no longer on the Reagan team, that [he] had betrayed the Reagan revolution—and especially the policy of deregulation."[28]

THE BUBBLE BURSTS

Then the bubble burst. Real estate deals turned sour. Texas was particularly hard hit. A big oil state, Texas' economy had expanded rapidly when oil prices shot through the ceiling during the 1970s. Then, in the early 1980s when the Regan recession reduced demand for petroleum, oil prices began to fall. Texas went from boom to bust. The real estate market collapsed. Texas S&Ls lost $25 billion in a few years. By 1988 it was estimated that it would take about $40 billion to clean up the S&L mess nation-wide. That's a lot of money, enough to give $5,633 to each of the 7.1 million American families with incomes below the federal government's poverty benchmark. It could finance 3.3 million scholarships of $12,000 each for college students.

But the $40 million was just the tip of the iceberg. In the summer of 1989, a new estimate of the cost of salvaging America's S&Ls was estimated to be between $157 and $300 billion. At a cost of $200 billion that's a potential tax bill of $3,125 for every American family. In July 1990, the General Accounting Office raised the estimated bailout cost at between $325 and $500 billion.[29]

The prime agent for dealing with the S&L mess is the Resolution Trust Corporation (RTC), a newly created arm of the Department of Treasury. So far it has seized 300 S&Ls and is poised to take over 250 more. The RTC sells off whatever valuable assets the banks have left, and tries its best to unload the remainder for which there are few buyers. Every year that a property remains unsold the cost of maintaining it— paying for insurance, maintenance and taxes—drives its recovery value down by about 20 or 30 percent. The RTC has already abandoned some property as a complete loss, like a $90 million shopping mall in Denver that costs more to keep open than it is worth.[30]

In an unprecedented move, the FDIC has been taking bankers to court, including President Bush's own son, Neil Bush. He is a former director of the Denver based Silverado S&L which collapsed in 1988 leaving the government with a $1 billion bill to cover bad loans based on insured depositors' money. Before Neil Bush became a member of Silverado's board of directors he received a $100,000 loan from Kenneth Good to invest in the commodities market with the understanding that if the investment went bad Neil Bush didn't have to pay the money back. When Neil Bush became a director at Silverado, he failed to alert his fellow directors of his special relationship with Good. Certainly, Bush was indebted to the man and this might easily be perceived as creating a conflict of interest if Good tried to do business with Silverado. In fact, Good was already a Silverado customer. A big one. He had borrowed a total of $14 million, and was having trouble paying it back. So Good asked Bush and the other directors to approve a restructuring of his loans. This was shortly after he had invested $3 million in one of Bush's companies. No mention was made of this fact at the board meeting. The restructuring was approved at a loss to the bank of about $13 million.[31]

Whatever the outcome of the case, Neil Bush and his $13 million fiasco is just small potatoes compared to other bankers like Don Dixon of Texas who stuck the government with a $1.3 billion in bad loans and fraudulent expenditures.

The savings and loan disaster is hands down the worst financial scandal in the nation's history. No one has yet suggested how the price to clean it up will be paid without running even larger budget deficits. And the Gramm-Rudman Balanced Budget Act of 1985 makes that difficult to accomplish even with creative accounting and moving programs off-budget.

One can imagine considerable pressure building to monetize the debt, though the Fed's strong stand against inflation would suggest it would refuse to go along. If this avenue is closed off, higher taxes in some form would seem to be just around the corner.

NOTES

[1]Stein, *Presidential Economics*, p. 347.

[2]"Foreign Funds in the U.S. Economy," *Real World Macro*, 6th ed., p. 47.

[3]Robert Heilbroner and Peter Bernstein, *The Debt and the Deficit* (New York: W.W. Norton and Company, 1989), pp. 32, 105.

[4]*Spokane Chronicle*, (Jan. 14, 1990), p. G1.

[5]Lester Thurow, *The Zero Sum Solution* (New York: A Touchstone Book, 1985). p. 259.

[6]Catherine Lynde, "Public Capital, Private Profits," *Real World Micro*, 2nd ed. (Menasha, WI: Economics Affairs Bureau, 1990),, p. 12.

[7]Lester Thurow, *The Zero Sum Solution* , p. 260.

[8]Greider, *Secrets of the Temple*, pp. 592-593.

[9]*Statistical Abstract of the United States* (1990), p. 794.

[10]Kevin Phillips, *The Politics of Rich and Poor* (New York: Random House, 1990), pp. 139-140.

[11]Ibid., p. 136.

[12]Ibid., p. 124.

[13]Frank Levy, *Dollars and Dreams* , pp. 122-125.

[14]Kevin Phillips, *The Politics of Rich and Poor* , p. 15.

[15]Robert Pollin, "Borrowing More, Buying Less," Real World Macro, 7th ed., p. 15.

[16]Kevin Phillips, *The Politics of Rich and Poor*, p. 90.

[17]Tim Wise, "What Did the Buyouts Buy?," in *Real World Micro*, 2nd ed., p. 38.

[18]Tim Wise, "Junk Bond Overdose," in *Real World Macro*, 7th ed., pp. 38-41.

[19]"Buyouts Humble American Sign," The Spokesman Review (Sept. 8, 1990).

[20]Robert Heilbroner and Lester Thurow, *Economics Explained* (New York: Touchstone Books, 1987), p. 148.

[21]Robert Lekachman, *Greed is Not Enough: Reaganomics* (New York: Pantheon

Books, 1981), p. ix.

[22]Kevin Phillips, *The Politics of Rich and Poor*, pp. 178-180.

[23]Ibid., p. 164.

[24]Ibid, pp. 156-7.

[25]Ibid., p. 213.

[26]Paul Pilzer and Robert Deitz, *Other People's Money* (New York: Simon and Schuster, 1989), p. 28.

[27]John Gallagher, "Good Ole Bad Boy," *Time*, (June 15, 1990), p. 42.

[28]quoted in Paul Pilzer and Robert Deitz, *Other People's Money* , p. 164.

[29]*The Washington Post National Weekly Edition*, (July 2-8, 1990), p. 7.

[30]Ibid., p. 10.

[31]Margaret Carlson, "It's a Family Affair," *Time,* (July 23, 1990), pp. 23-24.

Chapter 10

The Productivity Problem

A principle plank of Reagan's supply side economics was the claim that lower taxes for higher income individuals would result in massive investment in the economy and dramatic economic growth. That claim has proved false. The growth that has occurred has not been dramatic.

DECLINING ECONOMIC GROWTH

For the decade of the 1980s, growth of the GNP adjusted for inflation average 2.65 percent per year. In the 1950s the average was 3.98 percent; it was even higher in the 1960s—4.05 percent. In fact, the bad decade of the 1970s even outperformed the Reagan years, 2.83 average yearly growth compared to 2.65 percent. During the same period the growth rates of Japan, Canada, Finland, Turkey and Spain were greater. Even Great Britain managed to equal U.S. growth.

Even in the latter years of the 1980s (1985-89) when the deep recession of the early 1980s was but a bad memory, GNP growth in the U.S. averaged only 3.38 percent. That is just slightly higher than the growth rate of 1975-79, which averaged 3.22 percent. This hardly qualifies as an economic miracle, and is certainly far behind Japan's 4.2 percent, or Canada's 3.8 percent, or even little Spain's 4.6 percent for the same period.[1]

The rhetoric of Reaganomics aside, the principal reason for America's lackluster growth is the slow rate of growth in worker productivity. This is the real key to sustained economic growth, and if it does not pick up Americans will see their standard of living fall vis-a-vis other industrial nations. Already Switzerland and Japan enjoy a higher per capita

FIGURE 15

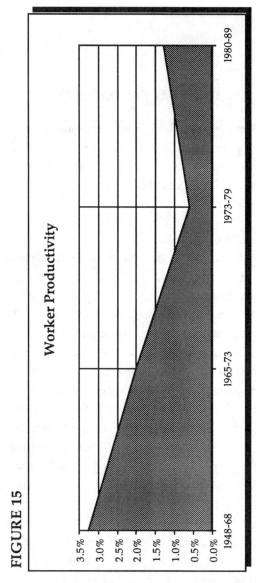

Worker Productivity

Source: Michael Mandel, "Is Productivity a Problem?" *Real World Macro*, 7th ed., p. 13; *Statistical Abstract of the United States (1990)*, p. 406.

share of GNP than the U.S., with Sweden and West Germany not far behind. What this reveals is that in Japan and Switzerland more is produced per worker than in the U.S. Their workers are more productive than ours. And if things keep going as they have in the past, West Germany and Sweden will soon catch up as and pass us as well.

DECLINING WORKER PRODUCTIVITY

Between 1948 and 1968 worker productivity in the U.S. measured in hourly output increased about 3.25 percent per year. Between 1965 and 1973 this rate dropped to about 2 percent. From 1973 to 1979 it fell to less than 1 percent. It is only in the last few years that worker productivity has enjoyed a modest increase to about 1.2 percent annually (see Figure 15). In fact, the best year was 1984 (2.6 percent). After that high watermark it was mostly downhill. By 1988 productivity had declined by nearly a full percentage point.

By comparison, the productivity of Japanese workers grew 4 percent annually through the 1970s, and continued to grow through the 1980s, though at a lower rate. Today Japanese workers are on average 20 percent more productive than American workers.[2]

Why have American workers become less productive? Some have blamed it on a decline in the work ethic, but there is little evidence that today Americans believe less in the work ethic than in the past. In fact, Americans work more hours per week than West Germans, and take fewer vacation days off than the Japanese. And due to the predominance of two-earner families, hours worked per family have continued to rise.[3] Many economists predicted just the opposite would happen. As worker incomes rose, the assumption was that they would choose to reduce the number of hours in the work week and pursue more leisure time activities. That hasn't occurred, and one reason may be a strong commitment to the work ethic. But if the work ethic has not declined then the cause of a fall in worker productivity must lie elsewhere.

One place to look is America's growing service sector. Two others are mining and construction where there has been a persistent decline in

FIGURE 16

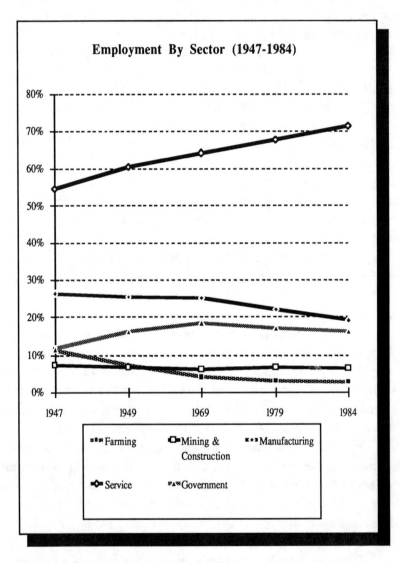

Source: Frank Levy, *Dollars and Dreams*, ch. 5.

worker productivity. Also there is the impact of the baby boomers once they entered the workforce, the defects of American management, the low savings rate of Americans, and the relatively modest role business accords government in the management of the economy.

GROWING SERVICE SECTOR

A larger proportion of America's economy is devoted to service than any of its international competitors. In 1947, employment in the service sector stood at 54.7 percent. By 1984, this had risen to 71.4 percent (see Figure 16).

This dramatic growth in the service sector of the economy is not very difficult to explain. As wage earners and businesses grew richer, they were better able to afford services to make their life or work easier.

Typically, when a family's income doubles it does not double its consumption of food or durable goods. A good deal of the additional income goes for services, like more medical care, eating out, vacations, etc. This, after all, is a major part of what people conceive as the good life.

Similarly, as the incomes of businesses grew larger, they too could afford more services—more lawyers, accountants, data processors and management consultants.[4] Indeed, over one third of the demand in the service sector today comes from business.

So one reason America has such a large service sector is that it can afford it. Other capitalist economies are moving in the same direction as they mature and become wealthier.

However, one difficulty with a large service sector is that services tend to be less productive than manufacturing or farming. A major reason for this lower productivity is that many services are labor intensive. Physicians can see only so many patients in a day. Barbers can cut only so many heads of hair.

Even in contexts where it might be assumed labor saving machinery in service oriented jobs might make a difference it often does not. In fact, it can sometimes lower productivity.

For example, the U.S. Postal Service spent $526 million on auto-mated equipment in 1989 to increase its mail processing efficiency. However the Postal Service continues to run a large deficit and has had to hire more workers to help process bar codes and nine-digit zips neces-sitated by the new machinery.

Nor has the use of computers in business always increased produc-tivity appreciably. In fact, additional resources and time have been consumed to train people to use computers. Digital Equipment Corpo-ration, a major supplier of small and medium sized main-frame computers to businesses and government, estimates that it devotes more classroom hours teaching its customers' employees how to use its equipment than Harvard, Yale, and Princeton needs to teach their combined student bodies.[5] Often the small gain in productivity has not outweighed the extra expense for computer training.

And increased productivity in one area is sometimes insufficient to overcome inefficiencies in others. In the late 1970s, American banks computerized their operations and installed automatic tellers. Even so, overall productivity declined. Why? Well, at the same time the banks used more computers they also hired more employees for other tasks, 21 percent more.[6] The productivity gains from the computers were not enough to compensate for the loss in productivity caused by the use of additional workers.

OIL AND MINING

Declining productivity in oil and mining are readily explained. We have less oil than before and it is more costly to extract what oil remains. Oil workers toil as hard as before, and may even use more advanced equipment, but because it takes more to extract less than before this translates into a fall in productivity.

The low productivity in mining is explained by additional burdens imposed by environmental regulations. Environmental regulations that require coal strip miners to repair the land after they have mined it necessitate additional workers to perform the same task. Not only does the coal have to be extracted, after it is hauled away the soil has to be replaced in the same order it was removed. This is not an argument for doing away with environmental regulations, it is simply a recognition that it costs more than before to perform the same work. This means a decline in productivity.

CONSTRUCTION

The construction industry has also suffered a decline in productivity, though explaining just why is difficult. Maybe fewer homes are being mass produced—less tract houses and more custom made homes. Perhaps it is because particular areas of construction have become inordinately costly, skewing the average.

However, some causes of lower productivity in construction are easily identifiable. In the late 1970s and early 1980s, over sixty nuclear power plants were abandoned before completion. Because of mismanagement and changes in safety regulations, the construction costs of nuclear power plants soared. Eventually, their cost rose so high—five plants in the state of Washington had a projected completion cost of $23.9 billion— there was no chance they could ever pay for themselves. Investors halted construction on several big plants and left them uncompleted. Such waste and inefficiency translates into lower productivity for the construction industry as a whole.

Yet, altogether the growing service sector, difficulties in oil and mining, and declining productivity in construction, still account for only about one-third of the overall decline in worker productivity in America.[7] To explain the remaining two-thirds we have to look elsewhere.

BABY BOOM WORKERS

One reason for declining productivity is the record number of new workers entering the economy in the 1970s. To be the most productive workers need the latest in machine technology to boost their output. This requires investment in new machinery and plants. Actually, investment was up during the 1970s, but productivity still lagged. The problem was that the unprecedented number of new workers also required unprecedented levels of investment to give them the equipment needed to be fully productive. It would have required about $60,000 in investment in new plants and equipment for each new worker to get the highest possible productivity out of the American workforce. With so many new workers, the expense was overwhelming. Few firms were willing to foot the bill.[8] In fact, there were nearly 30 million new workers added to the economy between 1965 and 1980. To provide all of them with the necessary machinery to maintain productivity would have required an investment of nearly two trillion dollars (1989 dollars), or about $120 billion per year. Not only was the expense too high, there was a powerful incentive to refrain from the investment. By the 1970s, with so many workers competing for jobs, real wages in many areas began to decline. With labor costs falling, it was cheaper for firms to hire more workers rather than invest in new equipment to increase output. The result was that the average worker lacked the necessary machinery to increase his or her productivity to the maximum. Average productivity declined accordingly.

AMERICAN MANAGEMENT

Another excellent place to look for a cause of declining productivity is the bloated white-collar segment of American business firms. Despite all its rhetoric about free enterprise being more efficient than government with its bloated bureaucracy, American business is highly bureaucratized compared to its foreign competitors. For example, we use far more office workers and managers to produce a car than do the Japanese. Japanese firms are thin in management and heavy in line workers. In American auto companies, for example, it is just the reverse. This appears to be a reflection of the management philosophy of American business, which places more importance on managers than on workers. This is an expensive philosophy because it is inefficient and reduces overall productivity.

A change in management philosophy can make a big difference, as National Steel discovered in 1982. Its steel plant at Weirton West Virginia was losing money, and National didn't have the funds to modernize it. So it offered to sell the plant to Weirton's employees. They took National up on the offer, secured a loan for $161 million, and began operations as a wholly worker owned company in January of 1984. Executives in the established steel companies "scoffed at the notion that employee ownership could succeed where traditional management could see only failure ahead."[9] Management at Weirton brought in consultants to introduce a worker participation plan to replace the old management centered hierarchy. Eight thousand employees organized into 117 participation groups met weekly to discuss and solve plant problems. Ways were found to cut production costs by $10.6 million. By the end of the year, Weirton was earning $41 for each ton of steel sold, higher than any of the six largest steel companies in the U.S. At the end of 1987, Weirton had managed fourteen consecutive quarters of profitability.[10]

Another problem with American management is that it is top-heavy with people trained as professional managers. Most have no technical training, or no production experience. Business schools turn out future executives who have been taught that the only real purpose of the corporation is to maximize stockholder earnings rather than producing inexpensive quality products.

The rise of mutual funds contributed greatly to this attitude. Prior to mutual funds, investors purchased particular stocks. While high earnings were desirable they always had to be balanced against risk. Large established firms may not have always paid the highest dividends, but they did have a proven track record. They were a safe investment. Newer companies might be growing fast and earning high profits, but they could also go bust. Their stock did not attract a lot of buyers.

The mutual fund was a way to get around the risk problem. Stocks were purchased from many different companies, some high yield high risk, other lower yield and low risk, and lumped together in a fund from which investors could purchase shares. Earnings from the fund depended

on the average performance of all its sundry stocks. Poor performance by
some high risk stocks was balanced out by an excellent performance by
others. In the mid-1960s mutual funds caught on, and by the 1980s
investments in mutual funds had risen from a lowly $78 million in 1958 to
$24 billion.[11]

The success of mutual funds put pressure on corporations large and
small to keep the value of their stock high. Since the mutual funds had
taken a good deal of the risk out of stock ownership, attention was
concentrated on high returns. Now the stock of established corporations
had to compete with the stock from new rapid growth firms. Risk was no
longer a major consideration. Instead, everything depended on high
yields. And if a corporation's stock didn't provide good returns, quarter
to quarter, the mutual funds would dump them for stocks with better
yields. This made it difficult for companies to invest profits in new plants
and equipment. If they used profits for investment rather than dividend
payments to stockholders, the attractiveness of their company's stock
would decline and they would have difficulty in the future selling more.
So an emphasis was placed on maximizing the net worth of stockholder
equity, and in business schools the idea was preached as gospel.

The difficulty is that concentrating on stockholder equity to the
neglect of nearly everything else is extremely short sighted. Long term
success depends on product quality and productive efficiency. Often this
requires using profits for investment in new technology rather than for
dividends to stockholders. It also means an appreciation of the importance
of the product produced. Sadly, the emphasis on stockholder equity has
favored the recruitment of managers with that orientation rather than
executives who understand something about the manufacturing of the
company's product. Over two-thirds of Japanese firms are headed by
CEOs trained as engineers or scientists.[12] In America, the ratio is
reversed. Only one-third have such training. Managers in Japanese corporations are more likely to understand, and have an appreciation for, the
importance of the manufacturing process and the product their company
produces than do American managers, and it shows up in the quality of the

products they sell. It is also reflected in the amount of corporate earnings plowed back into Japanese companies to keep them on the edge of the latest technology.

It should come as no surprise that America's outdated management philosophy has resulted in poor management decisions that have damaged the productivity of American industry. In both steel and autos, American executives refused to invest in modernizing their operations when their foreign competitors did so. American auto and steel workers were forced to get by with antiquated equipment while their counterparts in Japan and West Germany use the latest technology to produce cars and steel. American automobile manufacturers delayed modernization because the required investment would reduce profit margins. They were dominated by short-range thinking, pursuing quick profits at the expense of long term growth. Steel companies, on the other hand, made investments but not in steel. America's largest steel producer, U.S. Steel, concluded competition in the steel industry was too stiff and decided to move out of steel. Draining profits away from its steel operations, it purchased Marathon Oil and Texas Oil & Gas. By 1986, 75 percent of U.S. Steel's revenues came from its oil operations. It was now more an oil than a steel company. To reflect the change, the company changed its name to USX— the X having been its long standing stock exchange symbol.

Short sighted executives concentrating on high profits in the short term and forgoing the investment in new technology that would yield higher worker productivity and competitiveness in the longer term placed American workers at a distinct disadvantage. Deprived of the latest technology they couldn't be as productive as their Japanese or West German counterparts. In the end, many of them lost their jobs because their companies were unable to match the price and quality of the products of foreign competitors. Auto and steel plants were closed in Michigan, West Virginia, and Pennsylvania. Over a half million workers joined the lines of the unemployed.

LOW SAVINGS RATE

But even if America's business executives performed better and made the decision to invest for the future, where would the funds come from? American's have the lowest savings rate of any industrialized nation. West Germans save nearly 15 percent of their income. The Japanese save even more—20 percent. Americans save less than five percent. The corporate savings rate is higher, but not enough to make up the difference. When individual and corporate savings are lumped together, Americans still save much less than the Japanese or West Germans—one-third to fifty percent less. Unless Americans begin saving more, the capital for investment in new technology, the key to increased worker productivity, will not be available.

ROLE OF GOVERNMENT

The role of government in business is another big difference between the U.S. and its foreign competitors. Japan is the most extreme case. There, government coordinates economic development, teaming banks with venture capital to enterprising industries in a long term strategy to capture markets. Because the Japanese are not burdened with a huge military establishment or a military industrial complex, the government is able to devote a larger share of its budget to domestic scientific and engineering research. Also, the government has invested heavily in the Japanese educational system. Over the years, it has become one of the best in the world. Meanwhile, education in the U.S. continues to deteriorate to the point where it is now a national scandal.

In contrast, in the U.S. business is eager to use government to advance its ends, but hostile to government leadership and direction. The very idea of an industrial policy where government identifies potential growth markets, encourages banks to finance development in these areas, and supports research and development to advance useful technology, is anathema to the business community. The fear is that government will deprive business of its traditional independence, and force executives to make decisions that benefit the nation rather than their particular company. However, as two prominent economists observe:

> American enterprise has not learned how to organize its effort in a new setting that is global in scope, and where the traditional division between government and business is blurring. We may not like the emerging way of economic life, but it exists and must be taken into account when we inquire why we have fallen behind.13

The message is clear. American businessmen will have to change their attitude toward government involvement in the economy if they ever hope to compete effectively in the global marketplace.

TURNING THINGS AROUND

Turning things around will not be easy. The mentality of American business executives took decades to nurture and develop. Business schools have a great deal vested in the product they have created. It is unlikely they will admit their education has been defective and try something new. Most likely they will graduate the same type of business manager they have in the past. Corporate executives also have a great deal invested in the system as it is, especially as it rewards them handsomely even for an abysmal performance. They will doubtless be hostile to any change.

To ask Americans to save more and spend less, or to help them become better savers by tightening up credit, will not be popular. For business it means declining sales. For consumers it means accepting a stagnant or declining standard of living for a time in order to enjoy a higher standard of living in the future. There is no sign that our political leaders have either the foresight or courage to request such a sacrifice. Nor is there much evidence Americans would respond positively if the appeal were ever made.

Last of all, hostility to government leadership in nearly every area of society is ingrained in American culture. Certainly it is *deeply* ingrained in the business community. To expect Americans, or its business leaders, to suddenly endorse a leadership or even a partnership role for government in business is unrealistic.

So increasing worker productivity will not be easy. American business managers have become almost constitutionally short-sighted. Only in a few cases have large American corporations taken the long view and this was only when they were forced under extreme pressure by foreign competition to do so or face collapse.

For example, General Motors was typical of many large corporations in concentrating on marketing and finance rather than manufacturing excellence and productivity. It's management was inefficient and outmoded, as were most of its auto plants. Year after year it lost market share as Americans abandoned GM cars for imports from Japan and, later, domestic models from Ford and Chrysler who, in the mid 1980s, finally began to modernize their operations,streamline their management, and produce quality cars. GM was losing money everywhere except in its foreign plants in Europe where it produces the Opel and Vauxhall.

Then in 1988, Roger Smith, the CEO of GM, retired and Robert Stempel took the helm of the sprawling auto giant. Unlike Smith whose background was in finance and accounting, Stempel was an engineer who had pioneered technical innovations in transmissions and catalytic converters. He appreciated the production side of automaking and decided to turn the company around, mostly by outdoing the Japanese at their own game. Quality control and new equipment were brought to many GM plants. Also the management philosophy was changed, emphasizing teamwork over the old authoritarian hierarchy of the past. The biggest change was the company's $3.5 billion investment in the Saturn auto plant near Nashville, Tennessee. It is the most modern auto plant in America, brimming with the latest in robot technology. But perhaps the most significant change is in the mile long plant's management, which is even more team oriented than what can be found in Japanese factories. The new Saturn cars have received good reviews. They are of comparable or higher quality and lower priced. The cars are expected to compete well against the Japanese imports.[14]

But there are many other large corporations, like US Steel, which still follow the old philosophy, much to the detriment of the national economy. This suggests that turning things around may be very difficult in the short run. Perhaps even in the long run, too. If so, America will face a steadily declining standard of living vis-a-vis its international industrial rivals.

NOTES

[1]Data compiled from *Real World Macro*, 7th ed, p. 91; *U.S. Statistical Abstract* (1990), pp. 840-41.

[2]Michael Mandel, "Is Productivity a Problem?" *Real World Macro*, 7th ed., p. 13.

[3]Lester Thurow, *The Zero-Sum Solution*, pp. 140-141.

[4]Frank Levy, *Dollars and Dreams*, p. 85.

[5]Edward Tenner, "High-Tech Tantalus," *The Wilson Quarterly* (Summer, 1990), pp. 102-104.

[6]Lester Thurow, *The Zero Sum Solution*, p. 81.

[7]Robert Heilbroner and Lester Thurow, *Economics Explained*, p. 147.

[8]Lester Thurow, *The Zero-Sum Solution*, p. 84.

[9]John Hoerr, *And the Wolf Finally Came* (Pittsburgh: University of Pittsburgh Press, 1988), p. 449.

[10]Ibid., pp. 470-71, 449.

[11]David Halberstam, *The Reckoning*, p. 231.

[12]Lester Thurow, *The Zero Sum Solution*, p. 169.

[13]Robert Heilbroner and Lester Thurow, *Economics Explained*, p. 151.

[14]S.C. Gwynne, "The Right Stuff," *Time* (October 29,1990), pp. 74-84.

Bibliography

Allen, Frederick Lewis. "The Bull Market and the Crash of '29," in Paul Samuelson, Robert Bishop and John Coleman (eds.), *Readings in Economics*. New York: McGraw-Hill Book Company Inc., 1958.

Bennett, James and Thomas DiLorenzo. *Underground Government: The Off-Budget Public Sector*. Washington D.C.: Cato Institute, 1983.

Berry, Jeffrey. *The Interest Group Society*. Boston: Little, Brown, And Company, 1984.

Blewett, Steve. *A History of The Washington Water Power Company, 1889-1989*. Spokane, WA: The Washington Water Power Company, 1989.

Blumberg, Paul. *Inequality in an Age of Decline*. Oxford: Oxford University Press, 1981.

Brewster, Lawrence. *The Public Agenda*. 2nd ed. New York: St. Martin's Press, 1987.

Brownlee, Elliot "The American Way." *The Wilson Quarterly*, Spring, 1989.

Budget of The United States Government (1991). Washington DC: U.S. Government Printing Office, 1990.

"Buyouts Humble American Sign." *The Spokesman Review*, Sept. 8, 1990.

Burck, Gilbert and Charles Silberman. "What Caused the Great Depression." in Morton Grossman et. al. (eds.). *Readings in Current Economics*.Homewood, Illinois: Richard D. Irwin, Inc., 1958.

Camden, Jim. "'Low-end' scenario would drain Spokane." *Spokane Chronicle* , Aug 5, 1990.

Carlson, Margaret. "It's a Family Affair." *Time*, July 23, 1990.

El Mallakh, Ragaei. *Saudi Arabia: Rush to Development—Profile of an Energy Economy and Investment*. Baltimore: The Johns Hopkins University Press, 1982.

Fairchild Economic Resource Impact Statement (1989), prepared by 92d Cost Analysis Branch.

Fallows, James. *National Defense*. New York: Vintage Books, 1981.

Galbraith, John Kenneth. *Money: Whence It Came, Where It Went.* Boston: Houghton Mifflin, 1975.

—— *The Great Crash 1929.* Boston: Houghton Mifflin Company, 1961.

Gallagher, John. "Good Ole Bad Boy." *Time* , June 15, 1990.

Goldman, Marshal. *USSR in Crisis.* New York: W.W. Norton, 1983.

Greider, William. *Secrets of the Temple.* New York: Touchstone Books, 1987.

Halberstam, David. *The Reckoning.* New York: William Morrow and Company, 1986.

Heilbroner, Robert and Peter Bernstein. *The Debt and the Deficit.* New York: W.W. Norton and Company, 1989.

Heilbroner, Robert and Lester Thurow. *Economics Explained.* New York: Touchstone Books, 1987.

Heilbroner, Robert L. *The Worldly Philosophers.* New York: Simon and Schuster, 1961.

Hodgson, Godfrey. *America in Our Time.* New York: Doubleday & Company, 1976.

Hoerr, John. *And the Wolf Finally Came.* Pittsburgh: University of Pittsburgh Press, 1988.

Holesovsky, Vaclav. *Economic Systems: Analysis and Comparison.* New York: McGraw-Hill Book Company, 1977.

How Congress Works. Washington, D.C.: Congressional Quarterly Inc., 1983.

Hume, David. *Writings on Economics.* Edinburgh: Thomas Nelson & Sons, 1955.

Jones, Landon. *Great Expectations.* New York: Ballantine Books, 1980.

Kuttner, Robert. *The Economic Illusion: False Choices Between Prosperity and Social Justice.* Boston: Houghton Mifflin Company, 1984.

Lekachman, Robert. *Greed is Not Enough: Reaganomics.* New York: Pantheon Books, 1981.

Levy, Frank. *Dollars and Dreams.* New York: W. W. Norton and Company, 1988).

Light, Paul. *Artful Work: The Politics of Social Security.* New York:

Random House,1985.

—— *Baby Boomers*. New York: W.W. Norton, 1988.

Lowi, Theodore. *The End of Liberalism*. New York: W.W. Norton, 1979.

Lynde, Catherine. "Public Capital, Private Profits." Real World Micro, 2nd ed. Menasha, WI: Economics Affairs Bureau, 1990.

Mandel, Michael "Is Productivity a Problem?" *Real World Macro*, 7th ed. Menasha, WI: Economics Affairs Bureau, 1990.

Markovich, Denise and ronald Pynn. *American Political Economy: Using Economics with Politics*. Pacific Grove, CA: Brooks/Cole Publishing Company, 1988.

McConnell, Grant. *Private Power and American Democracy*. New York: Alfred A. Knopf, 1967.

Melman, Seymour. *The Permanent War Economy*. New York: Touchstone Book, 1985.

Milford, Lewis. *The Wages of War*. New York: Simon and Schuster, 1989.

Miller, John. "Washington's Magic Act." *Real World Macro*, 7th ed. Menasha, WI: Economics Affairs Bureau, 1990.

Moynihan, Daniel Patrick. "The Peace Dividend." *The New York Review of Books*, June 28,1990.

Pechman, Joseph. *Tax Reform*. 2nd ed. Washington, D.C.: The Brookings Institution, 1989.

Pelling, Henry. *American Labor*. Chicago: University of Chicago Press, 1960.

Phillips, Kevin. *The Politics of Rich and Poor*. New York: Random House, 1990.

Pilzer, Paul and Robert Deitz. *Other People's Money*. New York: Simon and Schuster, 1989.

Pollin, Robert. "Borrowing More, Buying Less." *Real World Macro,* 7th ed.Menasha, WI: Economics Affairs Bureau, 1990.

Polsby, Nelson. *Consequences of Party Reform*. Oxford:Oxford University Press, 1983.

Ransom, Roger. *Coping With Capitalism: The Economic Transformation of the United States 1776-1980.* Englewood Cliffs, New Jersey: Prentice-Hall, 1981.

Real World Macro. 5th ed. Somerville, MA: Economic Affairs Bureau, Inc., 1990.

Real World Macro, 6th ed. Somerville, MA: Economic Affairs Bureau, Inc., 1989.

Real World Macro, 7th ed..Menasha, WI: Economics Affairs Bureau, 1990.

Remnick, David "A Vast Landscape of Want." *The Washington Post National Weekly Edition,* May 28 - June 3, 1990.

"Research Report," *The Wilson Quarterly,* Summer 1990.

Ritter, Lawerence and William Silber. *Money.* 3rd rev. ed. New York: Basic Books, Inc., 1977.

Rustow, Dankwart. *Oil and Turmoil.* New York: W.W. Norton and Company, 1982.

Schwarz, John. *America's Hidden Success.* revised ed. New York: W.W. Norton, 1988.

Smith, Hedrick. *The Power Game* .New York: Ballantine Books, 1988.

Solomon, Ezra. *Beyond the Turning Point.* San Francisco: W.H. Freeman and Company, 1982.

Spokane Chronicle, Jan. 14, 1990.

Statistical Abstract of the United States (1990). Washington DC: U.S. Department of Commerce, 1990.

Stein, Herbert. *Presidential Economics.* 2nd ed. Washington, D.C.: American Enterprise Institute, 1988.

Stockman, David. *The Triumph of Politics.* New York: Avon Books, 1987.

Summers, Harry. *Vietnam War Almanac.* New York: Facts On File Publications, 1985.

Sutton, Howard. *Contemporary Economics.* Hinsdale, Illinois: The Dryden Press, 1976.

Tenner, Edward. "High-Tech Tantalus." *The Wilson Quarterly,* Summer, 1990.

Thurow, Lester. *The Zero Sum Solution.* New York: A Touchstone Book, 1985.

Tyler , Poyntz (ed.). *Securities, Exchanges and the SEC.* New York: H. W. Wilson Company, 1965.

Wanniski, Jude. *The Way the World Works.* New York: Simon and Schuster, 1978.

Weintraub, Sidney. *Our Stagflation Malaise.* Westport, Connecticut: Quorum Books, 1981.

Welfeld, Irving. *Where We Live.* New York: Simon and Schuster, 1988.

Wise, Tim. "Junk Bond Overdose." *Real World Macro,* 7th ed. Menasha, WI: Economics Affairs Bureau, 1990.

Wise, Tim. "What Did the Buyouts Buy?" in *Real World Micro.* 2nd ed. Menasha, WI: Economics Affairs Bureau, 1990.

Yarmolinsky, Adam. *The Military Establishment.* New York: Harper Colophon Books, 1971.

INDEX

Y

About the Author

Keith Quincy attended U.C.L.A. on a football scholarship where he received a B.A. in philosophy and a M.A. in political science. He earned his Ph.D in philosophy from the Claremont Graduate School. A former Fellow in the Institute in Higher Education, Claremont University Center, he taught philosophy at the University of California, Riverside and at the California Polytechnic Institute at Pomona before moving to the Pacific Northwest. Presently, he is Professor of Government at Eastern Washington University, and President of the Center for Education in Politics.

In addition to articles on political philosophy, he is the author of four books: *Coercion* (1976), *The Seamy Side of Government* (1979), *Hmong: History of a People* (1988 and 1990), and a novel—*Samuel* (1991)

He lives in the Marshall Creek Canyon outside of Spokane, Washington with his wife, Anna, three dogs and two thousand wild ducks and geese who claim squatter's right to their pond.